Immigration and Schooling

Redefining the 21st Century America

A Volume in
Critical Constructions: Studies on Education and Society

Series Editors
Curry Stephenson Malott, *West Chester University of Pennsylvania*
Brad J. Porfilio, *Lewis University in Romeoville, IL*
Marc Pruyn, *Monash University*

Critical Constructions:
Studies on Education and Society

Curry Stephenson Malott,
Brad J. Porfilio, and Marc Pruyn, Series Editors

Immigration and Schooling

Redefining the 21st Century America

edited by

Touorizou Hervé Somé
Ripon College

and

Pierre W. Orelus
*New Mexico State University,
Las Cruces, New Mexico*

INFORMATION AGE PUBLISHING, INC.
Charlotte, NC • www.infoagepub.com

Library of Congress Cataloging-in-Publication Data

A CIP record for this book is available from the Library of Congress
http://www.loc.gov

ISBN: 978-1-62396-892-2 (Paperback)
       978-1-62396-893-9 (Hardcover)
       978-1-62396-894-6 (ebook)

Printed in the United States of America

CONTENTS

PART II: LANGUAGE, MINORITY STUDENTS, AND ACADEMIC ACHIEVEMENT

PREFACE

Immigrants and Schooling in a Neoliberal Context

Carl E. James

Most of us are familiar with the narratives pertaining to immigrants—they are hardworking, resilient, and ambitious; willing to work at whatever jobs they can get; and highly motivated by remarkable aspirations. Also they possess a healthy sense of optimism and determination and see education as a means by which they, and more importantly their children, will be able to succeed in the society. Within this narrative is the notion that the United States is "a nation built by immigrants" (Irizarry & Kleyn, 2011). But as Irizarry and Kleyn (2011) also point out in their article: "Immigration and Education in the 'Supposed Land of Opportunity,'"

> A look back over time shows that the United States has a long-standing love-hate relationship with immigration. While many reflect fondly on how new-comers from earlier generations have shaped and contributed to our society, negative attitudes toward immigrants have always been present throughout our nation's history, and xenophobia, racism, and exclusion permeate the national dialogue around present-day immigrants. (p. 7)

Immigration and Schooling: Redefining the 21st Century America, pp. vii–xvii
Copyright © 2015 by Information Age Publishing

Within this "present-day" context, immigrants (most of whom have lived in the U.S. for many years), and even their American-born children, seem unable to surmount the immigrant categorization. In fact, as novelist Junot Diaz indicates, one never "stops being an immigrant" (Ratner-Arias, 2013, para. 6) Diaz, who immigrated to the United States from the Dominican Republic at age 6 and is today teaching creative writing at Massachusetts Institute of Technology, reveals:

> I certainly never stopped being one [an immigrant].... I think, most people have little experience about the internal lives of immigrants and the reality of immigration. We have lots of myths about it.... We assume that immigration is a deficiency that can be overcome, that there's some strange advance that one makes where one sheds this inadequacy to attain some sort of national purity. (para. 6)

The published sample of website responses to Diaz's claims reflect the attitudes and beliefs that those who talk about their own immigrant experiences (or that of others) can expect from people who steadfastly cling to notion of a welcoming, colorblind, postracial, and tolerant society. One posting is particularly instructive, and hence is worth quoting in full. The source who identifies him/herself as "sir3on, 78fan" writes:

> Juan may be right about a person who moves from another country. But this country has absorbed millions of immigrants from all over the world long before Juan arrived, and one of the things that stands out is that the first generation of most immigrant groups did its best to fit in and to think of themselves as american (*sic*) first and to work hard and proposer, and to teach their children to do the same. But we see a different phenomena (*sic*) now with the rise of the entitlement mentality, where some immigrant groups like latinos (*sic*), seem to want to think of themselves as Mexicans or people of whatever country they come from first, and Americans second. The irony of the situation is that they come seeking the prosperity economic freedom brings, but don't know enough to know that the lack of opportunity in their native land stemmed (sic) mostly from lack of economic freedom and so they tend to support politicians and policies that tend to bring here the same lack of opportunity they left home to escape.[1]

It is this prevailing attitude and presumption about today's immigrants—compared to their earlier counterparts—as not making efforts to "fit" into the society, not identifying as Americans, and having an "entitlement mentality" that this volume by Touorizou Hervé Somé and Pierre Wilbert Orelus seeks to address. With their contributors, Somé and Orelus report on the "present-day" situation of immigrants, their role in defining 21st century United States, and how they have engaged and navigated the structures of xenophobia, racism, language prejudice (or linguicism), and discrimination. They alert us to the ways in which immigrants and their children are exercising agency. They do so by making use of their social and cultural capital, nurtured by their immigrant drive and optimism, to resist marginalization and exclusion and eventually on their terms make their contributions to American society. So contrary to the narrative of today's immigrants being people who are social and economic liabilities, this relevant and timely volume tells of how the children of immigrant parents (in fact, second-generation Americans), and immigrants themselves (first-generation Americans) navigate and negotiate the systemic barriers and obstacles, and persevere with their schooling and education in their efforts to realize their own and/or their parents' ambitions of the American dream.

Ghiso and Campono (2013) write that "some of the most vulnerable populations in our school system are immigrant students, in particular those who endure systemic disadvantage due to a combination of their racialized identities, home language, poverty and undocumented status" (p. 255). Yet, ironically, it is in the school system that immigrants place their trust and confidence believing that as they become educated in the ways of the society—that is, learn "U.S. values, beliefs, and behaviors … [and] their role in American society" (Koo, Peguero, & Shekarkhar, 2012, p. 78)—they will acquire the social and cultural capital needed to effectively negotiate the societal structures and become accepted, fully participating members or citizens of the society. Yan Ciupak's (Chapter 2 of this volume) review of four decades of research on the assimilation process and educational attainment among children of immigrants indicates that factors such as historical context, social capital, bilingualism, differences between home and school cultures, and the students' connections to their ethnic background affected their academic performance and attainment—which were also mediated by the social constructs and related perceptions of the immigrant group. However, as critical theorists remind us, education and the socialization that takes place in the schooling process is structured according to the market imperatives of our capitalist system, which is advanced by neoliberalism (Porfilio & Malott, 2008).

It is useful, then, to reference neoliberalism because it provides a lens for viewing, or a framework for interpreting, the experiences, ambitions, and educational issues of the immigrants and their children that appear in this volume. Premised on the notion of individualism, democracy, competition, choice, tolerance, colorblindness, religious and cultural freedom, equality of opportunity, entrepreneurship, and globalization, neoliberalism is an ethos of social good by which the state operates (see Braedley & Luxton, 2010; Connel, 2010; Hursh, 2008), and which lures individuals into believing that they must take responsibility for their own life situation, care, and goals in ways that they see fit; for in doing so, and with existing choices and opportunities, they are able to shape the path toward realizing their ambitions. A "transnational political project," to use Wacquant's (2008) term, neoliberalism is premised on the principles of a market economy and related competition that allow individuals to freely pursue wealth on their own thereby avoiding the constraints of state-structured welfare. But in a context of structural inequity, "the resources and opportunities to which individuals have access, and concomitantly their freedom and choices, are inevitably structured by the economic and social conditions over which they have little or no control" (James, in press; see also Braedley & Luxton, 2010; Porfilio & Malott, 2008).

The common sense logic of neoliberalism, which serves to convince individuals of their responsibilities and shape their lives—in this case, immigrants and their children—means that they will attribute whatever social and economic circumstances in which they find themselves to their own actions, inadequacies, and poor choices, rather than to the structural inequities that generate limited, problematic, or useless choices. Indeed, as Luxton (2010) writes, this "perverse form of individualism"—"an obstinate and persistent belief that blames the victim by privatizing social problems" (p. 172)—has the potential to immobilize individuals, causing them to become resigned to their situation, having failed to see that they are both formed by and subjected to the prevailing values, norms, and practices of the economic, social, educational, and political structures of society. Or as Orelus (Chapter 1 in this volume) discusses, in their search for home, and in the face of xenophobia, racism, and marginalization, immigrants will try to assimilate into mainstream society, move to neighborhoods to live with people of similar racial and cultural background, find solace in religious institutions, and/or regularly visit their "homeland" to regenerate their sense of belonging to somewhere. Nevertheless, none of these coping strategies will efficaciously create that sense of belonging denied to them in a socially and economically stratified society. The situation for American-born youth should be concerning, in that as Orelus writes, some may seek that sense of belonging in gangs. There are gendered differences that are useful to consider; for as Koo et al. (2012) report in their study of "school victimization" among African American, Latino, and Asian American public school students, such "victimization is a serious social and educational problem," particularly among male students (p. 90).

The personal and societal dilemmas (or costs) notwithstanding, government and business bureaucrats are well aware of the benefits of immigration to the country. To this end, efforts are made to ensure that only "qualified" people who "fit in" are allowed to settle in the country, where through their transnational activities, engagement in the workforce, and commitment to education as a means to succeed in their new society among other ways, they contribute to the social, cultural, and economic well-being of the society—things that help to advance the neoliberal agenda. Indeed, individuals who willingly leave family and friends to settle in a new country, and with their optimism, faith, determination, and willingness to do whatever it takes to realize their ambitions in a new country, help to propagate and maintain the culture of competition, individual responsibility, healthy work ethic, and entrepreneurship, not only within their workplaces, families, and particular immigrant communities, but also in the society generally. And not yet disillusioned, embittered, or worn-out from years of fighting the inequitable social and economic structures, we can expect that children, like their immigrant parents, will strive to achieve the goals through education as inspired by their parents. This is why, as numerous studies indicate, that first- (children who immigrated) and second- (born to immigrant parents) generation students tend to do better educationally than those of other generations (James, 2012). In this regard, it is important for scholars to constantly report on the experiences of students of immigrant backgrounds to ensure that the school system is responsive to their needs, interests and aspirations, thereby keep alive what they expect to attain through their education.

Rudi-Ann Miller's story, as reported in the *New York Times* by Fernanda Santos, is a useful reference here (Santos, 2012). Having completed seventh grade in Jamaica in the Caribbean, Rudi-Ann immigrated to New York to join her parents and "to live her parents' American dream." Accordingly, her parents enrolled Rudi-Ann in Stuyvesant High School in New York, which one of her father's work colleagues described as "the best New York City high school," and her mother's cousin, knowing this, with surprise, commented: "You have to be Chinese or Indian to get there." A Black co-worker further said: "the exam is built to exclude blacks because it's heavy on math, and black people can't do math." In fact, Santos writes that Rudi was one of 40 Black students out of the school's 3,295 students,[2] and a significant proportion, "about three-quarters of Stuyvesant's students are immigrants or children of immigrants." We might ask here, why is it that immigrants or children of immigrants are over-represented in the school? Is it that they are more academically well-prepared for these schools' programs, or that they do better on entrance tests, or compared to their other American counterparts, do better in side-stepping matters—such as those related to their "foreignness," xenophobia, race, and racism—that would otherwise serve as impediment to their achievements?

Take for instance the story of Steve, son of Trinidadian parents, whose "desire to succeed and achieve at the highest level was what drove [him]" (Garrod, Smulyan, Power, & Kilkenny, 2002, p. 103). A straight A student, he revealed that while his parents did not deter him from identifying as Black, they encouraged him not to be bogged down by or get entangled with identity issues. As Steve explained, they were "strict parents who focus on education, not 'the man' keeping them down" (Garrod, Victoria, Robinson, & Kilkenny, 2002, p. 103). Steve's teachers also contributed to the idea of him developing a distance from Blackness. His words were: "The counselors at school lauded me.... The teachers commented on how strong a character I was to overcome the stigma in black society that to be smart is to act white" (p. 103). This liberal notion communicated by parents and teachers, that race is irrelevant to student's identification—essentially, a tenet of colorblindness—paradoxically operates to, on the one hand, remind the students of their minoritized status within the society, and on the other hand, to inculcate in them that they are different from the other minority students—in Steve's case, that he is not Black like the rest of his peers. Colorblindness, then, seems to be a crucial element of the social and cultural capital that students of color need to cultivate and employ in their bid to successfully navigate and negotiate the educational system and attend their goals.

Here, I think of Angela and Zura, two of four African immigrant girls, who, according to Okwako (Chapter 4, this volume), were high-achieving students—Angela more so. Like Rudi-Ann and Steve, they employed strategies of achievement that, as Okwako contends, "in conventional terms demonstrated that in some ways they possessed the valued cultural capital necessary for school success." Accordingly, compared to their counterparts, Angela and Zura were able to effectively navigate the school system by using their acquired "knowledge of the operational structure" of the schooling system to access available opportunities, attain high grades (particularly to be able to get into university or college), take advantage of the necessary material and social resources (like social networks fostered through club membership), and develop relationships with their teachers. Moreover, to quote Okwako, these "two academically proficient students were very involved within the mainstream life in their school. They participated in school activities, had friends—American and non-American, and they embraced many of the mainstream norms of schooling." What is evident in these students' stories is the level of "conformity" to the mainstream—that is, adherence to the values, norms, language, customs and behaviors of the society structured by middle class Eurocentrism—that is required for these children of immigrant parents to do well in the existing school system. As such, the system remains intact.

To survive or succeed in the system, therefore, seems to require engaging in organized resistance to stereotyping, alienation, marginalization, and miseducation that are perpetuated by the education system. In Chapter 5: "Challenging a Troubling Miseducation," Shami demonstrates how Arab Americans resisted by exercising agency to protect themselves from negativities such as bullying, racial threats, racial profiling, and being told to "go home," which forced them to hide their Arab heritage, especially following 9/11 when they became acutely aware of their difference. These students' activism, writes Shami, "were motivated through connections with their Arab and non-Arab communities which helped to enhance or increase their awareness, education, personal growth, and intellectual and spiritual capacity" (p. 184), and their "sense of justice, moral responsibility, identity and ethnic pride, and faith-based values" (p. 185). These features are in keeping with what Yosso (2005) identifies as "community cultural wealth"— that "array of knowledge, skills, abilities and contacts" that are nurtured by racialized families and communities, which they utilize "to survive and resist macro and micro-forms of oppression" (p. 77).

A number of the chapters in this volume provide evidence of the ways in which neoliberalism operates to determine the educational trajectories of students. In fact, in their role as "institutional gatekeepers" of opportunities (Okwako), teachers play a pivotal role in structuring and supporting the learning process for students with culturally relevant curriculum content, pedagogical approaches, and classroom practices. But as Somé-Guiébré illustrates, in attempts to "mainstream" new immigrant students and accommodate their needs, teachers, possibly innocently, will place students of the "same" background together. One possible explanation for this practice is the idea that the group bears responsibility to help, or look after, each other. The case of Sally, a fifth grader, is instructive. Sally, who was a new student with limited fluency in English, was placed with the two other African peers in her class who were much more fluent in English. According to Somé-Guiébré, the resulting unequal power dynamics among the students—Sally relying on her peers for translation and her peers feeling pressured in their role as translators—damaged their self-esteem, contributed to tension among them, and for Sally, self-marginalization to resist the burden of the "power relationships" she was experiencing. Of course, in a Eurocentric education system based on monoglossic principles,[3] the linguistic and cultural capital that facility with English provides is not only a source of pride, but also a signal that students who possess this cultural capital are likely to do well in school. Therefore, expectations that students of the same language and ethnic background are in a position to, or should, help one another have worrying implications for their social and emotional well-being and educational performance.

Furthermore, the current approach to working with English language learners (ELLs) is failing to help these students to become productive members of society. Even in situations where students should be able to associate with each other and benefit from the support they could receive from each other, evidence suggests that segregated grouping in classrooms, curriculum content, pedagogical approaches, and assessment (or testing) programs in schools conspires to alienate them from their learning process by the ways in which teaching–learning is structured. Ruiz's account (Chapter 7) of the Spanish-speaking students who needed special supports in order to meet the testing requirements of the No Child Left Behind (NCLB) program not only reminds us of the limits of standardized testing, but also of the ways in which testing is handled—for instance, teaching the students as a homogeneous group and having them repeatedly take sample tests through a process of drilling. This approach to facilitating learning among ELLs can often lead to situations in which students feel stigmatized and as a consequence develop low self-esteem and a sense of inability to succeed in school. Clearly, reform is needed if schools are to be responsive to the language, abilities, and learning styles of their diverse student population. The administration of standardized tests, as Ruiz explains, is stressful for both teachers and students and as such, takes the joy out of teaching and learning. Evidently, testing does not help to build positive teacher–student relationships that are vital to the learning process. The irony is that the very students that teachers are trying to support through such assessments and related instructions are the ones who suffer the most. An added issue is that while students may have learned conversational language within a short time of arriving in the English environment, they may need up to five years to become proficient in academic language specific to school disciplines (Cummins, 2011).

Ruiz recommends that classrooms should be sites where students are integrated, where dialogue among them is promoted, and their languages encouraged as they interact with each other. Li (Chapter 6) concurs, suggesting that bilingual and bicultural literacy among students can be done by integrating multiple voices into the curriculum and promoting intercultural relationships. Such an approach teaches students to value language and appreciate bilingual abilities, and it helps to level the power dynamics in classrooms. Moreover, as Li, in Chapter 6, contends, getting away from the monolingual and/or monoglossic framework employed in schools— where English is considered the language for school and the student's first language the one for home—would help to address cultural discontinuity in students' experiences. In such a schooling context where language supports and access to culturally relevant learning are not provided by the schools—a consequence of which is likely low educational attainment— have understandably led some parents to supplement their children's education by, for example, sending them for private tutoring. Having to meet the expectations of parents and the demands of both school and private lessons contribute to increased workloads and pressure to succeed academically.

CONCLUSION

Most immigrant parents and their children strongly believe that education opens up possibilities and pathways to opportunities for social mobility and full participation in society. To this end, they exercise agency using their social, cultural, linguistic, and psychological skills while drawing on familial resources and social networks. But as Gueye and Lalonde (Chapter 8) have shown, based on their experiences teaching American and Canadian college students, race and accent (and I infer gender) played a role in how the students read their bodies and their interest in issues pertaining to race, equity, social justice, and globalization. These two college professors' experiences point to what immigrants in these two societies are up against—especially when English is not their first language, or they speak English with an accent (a non-American English accent, that is), and when their skin color, clothing, religious practices, and/or other attributes mark them as immigrants. These constructs of immigrants and reactions to them are well represented by the stories told by Gueye and Lalonde. Students saw the Black African-born professor's interest in race as "her thing," while the White American-born professor's interest was described as "her passion" (see also James, 2001), These reactions reflect the tendency, especially among Whites, to read race as a mainstay in the ideas and communications of people of color (hence, they are often thought of as biased and not objective), while for Whites this is not the case. This can be considered to be a product of White privilege (see Lensmire et al., 2013). In the words of Gueye and Lalonde: "Not only is race and whiteness as an empty signifier implicated in these differing students' responses, but language also plays a part, in relation to speaking English with a foreign accent ... versus speaking 'American' English without said accent" (p. 241).

Evidently, as represented in this volume, in 21st century United States, the neoliberal ethics of individualism, democracy, tolerance, race neutrality, and equality of opportunity that regulate and normalize the social, cultural, economic, and political discourses and practices of the society are not helping to fashion the welcoming society for immigrants and their families, as it might have done decades earlier Nevertheless, immigrant families and their children remain resilient, patient, and longsuffering. For as Yosso (2005) reasons, six dynamic interrelated forms of capital—aspirational, navigational, social, linguistic, familial, and resistant—that families and communities provide their youth of color help them to "maintain hopes and dreams for the future, even in the face of real and perceived barriers" (p. 77), imagine possibilities "beyond their present circumstances" (p. 78), and navigate institutional constraints and structural barriers. Moreover, according to the United States Census Bureau (2008): "Currently, 20% of all youth in U.S. schools have at least one immigrant parent; by 2030 the number of youth in immigrant families in the U.S. school system is expected to rise to 33%." Hence, it is imperative to address the issues that students from immigrant families are facing, because, as Koo and colleagues continue to point out, "they are part of this country's future: its parents, its labor force, its leaders, and its voters" (p. 93).

NOTES

1. Comment on Sigal Ratner-Arias (2013). http://www.huffingtonpost.
    com/2013/09/19junot-diaz-immigration_n_3954792.html?n...
2. Santos (2012) also writes that Asians "make up 72.5 percent of
    Stuyvesant's student body (they are 13.7 percent of the city's overall
    public school population), a staggering increase from 1970, when
    they were 6 percent of Stuyvesant students, according to state en-
    rollment statistics. Black then, white students made up 79 percent
    of Stuyvesant's enrollment; this year, they are 24 percent, and 14.9
    percent systemwide. Hispanic students are 40.3 percent of the
    system. Currently, they make up 2.4 percent of Stuyvesant's enroll-
    ment, while blacks, who make up 32 percent of the city's public
    school students, are 1.2 percent" (para. 6–7).
3. Ofelia Garcia (2009) talks of monoglossic ideologies of bilingualism
    and bilingual education in which a child's languages are treated as
    separate and whole, and his/her two languages as "bounded auton-
    omous systems" (p. 7).

REFERENCES

Braedley, S., & Luxton, M. (2010). *Neoliberalism and everyday life*. Montreal, Quebec:
    McGill-Queen's University Press.
Connell, R. (2010). Building the neoliberal world: Managers as intellectuals in a
    peripheral economy. *Critical Sociology, 36*(6), 777–792.
Cummins, J., (2011). *Teaching English language learners*. Retrieved from http://www.
    etfo.ca/resources/researchforteachers/pages/default.aspx
Diaz, J. (2013). Junot Diaz on immigration. *Huffington Post*. Retrieved from http://
    www.huffingtonpost.com/2013/09/19/junot-diaz-immigration_n_3954792.
    html
Garcia, O. (2009). *Bilingual education in the 21st century: A global perspective*.
    Chichester, UK: Wiley-Blackwell.
Garrod, A. C., Smulyan, L., Powers, S. I., & Kilkenny, R. (2002). *Portraits of ado-
    lescents: Identity, relationships, and challenges* (4th ed.). Boston, MA: Allyn &
    Bacon.
Ghiso, M. P., & Campano, G. (2013). Coloniality and education: Negotiating dis-
    courses of immigration in schools and communities through border thinking.
    Equity & Excellence in Education, 46(2), 252–269.
Hursh, D. (2008). Raising false fears: Hijacking globalization to promote neoliberal
    education policies. In B. Porfilio & C. Marlott (Eds.), *The destructive path
    of neoliberalism: An international examination of urban education* (pp. 23–40).
    Rotterdam, the Netherlands: Sense.

Irizarry J. G., & Kleyn T. (2011). Immigration and education in the "supposed land of opportunity": Youth perspectives on living and learning in the United States. *The New Educator,* 7(1), 5–26.

James, C. E. (2001). "I've never had a black teacher before." In C. E. James & A. Shadd (Eds.), *Talking about Identity: Encounters in race, ethnicity and language* (pp. 150–167). Toronto, Ontario: Between the Lines.

James, C. (2008). Immigrant parents and their educational expectations of their children: Struggles, contradictions and paradoxes. In B. Porfilio & C. Marlott (Eds.), *The destructive path of neoliberalism: An international examination of urban education* (pp. 103–122). Rotterdam, The Netherlands: Sense.

James, C. (2012). *Life at the intersection: Community, class and schooling.* Halifax, Nova Scotia: Fernwood.

James, C. E. (in press. Winter, 2015). Beyond education, brains and hard work: The aspirations and career trajectory of two Black young men. *Alternate Routes: A Journal of Critical Social Research.*

Koo, D. J., Peguero, A. A., & Shekarkhar, Z. (2012). The "model minority" victim: Immigration, gender, and Asian American vulnerabilities to violence at school. *Journal of Ethnicity in Criminal Justice*, 10(2), 129–147.

Lensmire, T. J., McManimon, S. K., Dockter Tierney, J., Lee-Nicholas, M. E., Casey, Z. A., Lensmire, A., & Davis, B. M. (2013). McIntosh as synecdoche: How teacher education's focus on white privilege undermines antiracism. *Harvard Educational Review*, 83(3), 410–431.

Luxton, M. (2010). Doing neoliberalism: Perverse individualism in personal life. In S. Braedley & M. Luxton (Eds.), *Neoliberalism and everyday life* (pp. 163–183). Montreal, Quebec: McGill-Queen's University Press.

Porfilio, B., & Malott, C. (2008). Introduction: The neoliberal social order. In B. Porfilio & C. Malott (Eds.), *The destructive path of neoliberalism: An international examination of urban education* (pp. xvii–xxix). Rotterdam, The Netherlands: Sense.

Ratner-Arias, S. (2013, September 19). Junot Diaz on immigration: "I'm not certain that anyone stops being an immigrant." *Huffington Post*. Retrieved from http://www.huffingtonpost.com/2013/09/19/junot-diaz-immigration n 3954792.html

Santos, F. (2012, February 25). To be Black at Stuyvesant High. *New York Times*. Retrieved from http://www.nytimes.com/2012/02/26/education/black-at-stuyvesant-high-one-girls-experience.html?_r=0

United States Census Bureau. (2008). *Current population survey.* Washington, DC: Author.

Wacquant, L. (2008). *Urban outcasts: A comparative sociology of advanced marginality.* Cambridge, UK: Polity Press.

Yosso, T. J. (2005). Whose culture has capital? A critical race theory discussion of community cultural wealth. *Race Ethnicity and Education*, 8(1), 69–91.

INTRODUCTION

Touorizou Hervé Somé

This book deals with the school experiences of immigrant children of latter days, for lack of a better term. It is intuitive to assume that these students would have a harder time navigating the school system than former immigrants who were mainly from Western Europe. This difficulty arises not so much because of the difference in time, but because of their different racial and national origins and the new economy.

This is not to say that all the children of European immigrants made it equally in the educational system. Now, more than ever, it is a fact that racial and national origins complicate the school experiences and outcomes of recent arrivals. Immigrants from Europe had their struggles, however specific they could be to each national group. However, the Euro-immigrants had a leg up in terms of integration and moving forward as they could at least blend into the mainstream racial tide (Nieto, 1992). Immigrants of other races are branded as foreigners; it does not matter how long they have been living in the United States. The best they can do is to be dubbed honorary guests (Lee, 2005). They are always visible in a way that makes the school experiences of their sons and daughters less seamless. The exception is Asian students, who are often stereotypically seen as the desirable students.

Research about the school experiences of the newcomer immigrant child in the United States is in short supply. Little is known about how they

Immigration and Schooling: Redefining the 21st Century America, pp. xix–xxvi
Copyright © 2015 by Information Age Publishing

navigate the school system and how they relate to the adults in the school building and how they construct their identities and strategize ways to both survive the system and make the best of their school experiences. Also, there is little research on how they live "la différence habitée" (Paré, 2004), the lived difference. When research attempts to capture the school experiences of these students, there seems to be an irresistible attempt to lump them together as if they all went about adaptation in the same way. This is true whether students are in K–12 or college (Some, 2012). There is a danger in not looking at the concept of immigrant as a notion in need of being situated in time and space. It is common for researchers to lump all immigrants together, beginning with the descendants of the first pilgrims, to the Chinese and Vietnamese, all the way to the recent immigrants from Africa, the Middle East, and Eastern Europe. However, by making this mistake, one cannot account for all the complexities involved in the concept of immigrant student.

There has been an influx of immigrant students in the American educational landscape, forcing the United States to contend with issues for which it is poorly prepared. Looking at the push and pull factors, it is not a stretch to say that the problems of other nations have become America's problems. This may be the reason for the rather narrow approach to the issue of immigrant students (Mulu et al., 2008). However, Ogbu (1988) developed a typology of the immigrant students, where he predicted better academic outcomes for the voluntary minority students. According to him, they embrace unproblematically the school ethos and work ethic of the mainstream. This is to the detriment of the involuntary minorities who reject schooling. They would tend to see school ethos and work ethic as culturally hegemonic. Such a view could be challenged in light of the actual changes that take place in the economy, family structure, spirit of the time, and overall social change (Ciupak, Chapter 2, this volume).

Suarez-Orozco (1987) was once a staunch supporter of Ogbu's stance that resistance of involuntary minorities to schooling in the U.S. is prompted by the type of power relationship that governs the stratified American society. In this view, the voluntary minorities were constructed as less of a challenge in educational terms. However, in their recent book, *Children of Immigration*, Carola Suarez-Orozco and Marcelo M. Suarez-Orozco (2002) contend that the voluntary minority immigrants' educational trajectory is as less happily predictable. This student population is crossing the best of times, but it is also in for the worst outcomes. They are liable to drop out of school, and they can see their dreams for a better future ruined. Students from this background can also magnify the already high prison rate of minorities in the American judicial system, regardless of their motivation compared to their non-minority counterparts. The rosy picture of the voluntary immigrant happily taking advantage of the opportunities available in this bountiful country is indeed losing currency in the face of stark realities. Among other variables, structural barriers in society and school factors (Ogbu & Simons, 1998) may be the culprits.

THE BOOK

This book captures the school experiences of the most recent immigrants. They were members of societies from parts of the world other than Western Europe, and they have been coming into the country in great numbers. This book gives a sense of what it means to be an immigrant student and a scholar at this particular point in time marked by school reforms that inevitably touch upon the lives of immigrant students. No doubt, these times of economic hardships are etched with a resurgence of anti-immigrant sentiments. It is important to stay clear of the tendency to subsume all voluntary immigrants under the same category. Contributors are clearly aware of the fact that school experiences of students are shaped along the lines of race, language, culture, ethnicity, gender, social class, nationality, sexual orientation, caste, and disability. Educational macropolicies and school practices grounded in teachers' deep-seated beliefs are also crucial factors in accounting for immigrant schooling outcomes. The contributions, mainly empirical in outlook, bring a whole new explanatory power to bear on the school experiences of immigrant students.

This volume is unique in the sense that it makes the case that all immigrant students, voluntary or involuntary, are at risk of failing. Espousing a capacity model, it celebrates culturally responsive practices. It challenges the notion that immigrant students bring with them deficits that severely limit their school outcomes. Taking a look at diversity from the perspective of equity and social justice, the systemic parameters such as state policies, overt curriculum, covert curriculum, socioeconomic status, and language barriers, it laments ingrained practices in our schools that have been debunked, yet die hard. There is the tendency to contain the explanation of the school experiences of immigrant students within the narrow parameters of cultural or economic factors, macropolicies mandated by the government, or individual factors of the students and their families. While there is a modicum of truth in each one of these perspectives, it is necessary to put together these factors in order to complicate the picture and provide avenues for new reflections about how to educate immigrant children.

OVERVIEW OF CHAPTERS

In Chapter 1, "In Search of a Place Called Home: The Linguistic, Cultural, and Socioeconomic Dislocations of Immigrants and Transnationals of Color," Pierre W. Orelus analyzes the concept of home, placing it in a transnational context. Specifically, Orelus pries open the complexity of home, pointing out that it cannot accommodate any singular definition. It is context-specific. That is, home can mean different things to different people depending on their life experiences and circumstances. They include their linguistic, sociohistorical, political, cultural, and geographical contexts. Orelus goes further to link the concept of home to community and memory, arguing that they are intertwined. Finally, he contends that for immigrants and transnational subjects who left their native land when they were very young, or who have been living in another land for decades, home can be a very complex notion for them to grapple with, as many may feel they have multiple homes or do not have any home.

In Chapter 2, "Education of Immigrants' Children: A Review of Four Decades of Empirical Research in the United States, 1965–2011," Yan Z. Ciupak provides a condensed look at the education of immigrant students. It goes back to 1965, a watershed in American immigration policy, after the long night of ostracism and quotas imposed upon certain nationalities. In 1882, the Chinese Act prohibited the Chinese from entering the country, and in 1924 the Oriental Act targeted Japanese Americans and immigrants.

Ciupak highlights schools as an agency for the reproduction of privileged groups and the transmission of intergenerational privileges. This line of inquiry, powerful as it is, errs on the side of viewing "difference along a narrowly constructed Black–White dichotomy" (p. 1) in its narrow focus on African American and Caucasian students. Ciupak shows a clear trajectory, whereby this bias is changing as diversity has brought schools to ponder "research questions related to children and families who are relatively new to American schools" (Shami, this volume, p. 2).

Ciupak argues that the bulk of research on immigrant education is geared towards the performance of immigrant students attending American public schools, namely secondary education, noting that evidence is encouraging, in spite of the social and economic problems immigrants are grappling with. This is not to say that all immigrants are equal in this regard. She uses the cultural, ecological theory of John Ogbu to account for this differential achievement. Other researchers have capitalized on culture and language or ethnic language maintenance to explain school achievement in addition to family background and social capital. The production of social identities has also been a powerful explanatory factor in immigrant students' achievement, even if the proponents of this approach hail from all directions. Ciupak closes the chapter with difficult questions, insisting on the necessity of looking beyond the American borders as transnationalism and global citizenship are the order of the day. "All these new global and domestic economic and political environments are closely affecting the immigrant children's experiences and, therefore, should illuminate our research" (p. 12).

In Chapter 3, Somé-Guiébré addresses the issue of alienation of immigrant students from peers and teachers, and how they struggle in the classroom due to their inadequate command of the English language. The classroom, and the school environment at large, is often not a welcoming place for them because of poor English skills. The English language learners are physically and emotionally separated from their native English speakers. Pulling students out of mainstream classes for ESL courses seems to be a poor substitute for their English language inadequacy. To make matters worse, because of classroom instruction and the implicit curriculum, namely, the unvoiced low expectations of teachers at play, English language learners receive the subliminal signal that they are the "other." All of this takes place in spite of the efforts of teachers who mean well, but whose good intentions ultimately backfire. Thus, immigrant students experience an unintended discrimination and feel a profound disconnect between themselves and their peers and teachers. In turn, they look inwardly to their homes and anything familiar to them as a free space and a safe haven.

In Chapter 4, "Conceptualizing Smartness: Using Social and Cultural Capital to Explain Academic Achievement Among a Group of African Immigrant Girls," Betty Okwako grapples with the issue of academic achievement among a group of African immigrant girls, a seldom-researched group among immigrant students, as she contends. Okwako laments the dearth of studies documenting the school experiences of African students in the United States as they navigate the school system. The four girls in her empirical study all share an immigrant background, yet because they come from different social and economic backgrounds, they end up achieving different academic outcomes. She concludes that cultural capital, social capital, and the idiosyncratic definition of success of these girls are crucial in how well they achieve on the scholastic plan.

In Chapter 5, "Challenging a Troubling Miseducation: Arab Americans in American Schools and Universities," Muna Jamil Shami casts light on the experiences of one of the underrepresented groups, Arab American students in formal and informal education settings, to direct our attention to the risk of fracture stalking the plurality that is foundational to the American society. Shami signals that America does not walk its talk of democracy, and because "[s]ocial issues are mirrored in the schools," it follows that "the battle of the day is the deepening of democracy" and that

schools and universities are inevitable battlegrounds for competing interests. Counterintuitively, from the survey administered to Arab American youths, schools are the most restricted spaces of discourse in the U.S., alongside

> Hollywood movies and television, school classrooms and textbooks, the news media and university classrooms and course readings. (p. 1)

The author maintains that there is a gross mis-education of America about Arabs and Islam—even more so after 9/11. Shami argues that it is a serious mistake to allow this to endure and still think that America is a land of democracy and cultural pluralism.

> The survey participants were asked to share a personal story of growing up Arab American. More than 50 respondents shared stories where they felt different, where they did not fit in or where they were out of place. Many participants shared experiences where they felt marginalized, and several used humor to tell their stories. (p. 9)

If some students exercised agency and developed an identity as Arabs through interacting with a community of Arab Americans, the bulk of the students fell prey to discrimination and feelings of embarrassment. Some feel the need to erase or stifle aspects of their identity, seeking to fit in, whatever the cost. The school that should be a space free of discrimination is unfortunately the place where the curriculum is biased against Arab Americans. Insensitive teachers still care little about being culturally responsive to students. In conclusion, Shami makes a clarion call for broadening public discourse and recentering freedom and pluralism, the sine qua non for moving democracy forward.

In Chapter 6, "Best Approaches to Literacy Instruction to English Language Learners: Cultural Conflicts and Compromises," Li reflects on best approaches to literacy, targeting mainstream teachers who become ESL teachers in spite of themselves. Li highlights the inevitable tensions born out of the encounter of mainstream teachers in America who are hard set in their beliefs in what counts as literacy and parents of minority students, Chinese immigrants specifically, who are molded by different cultural models. This encounter is fraught with clashes that can have a huge repercussion on student achievement. Li laments the dichotomization of literacy practices that cause a cultural discontinuity, therefore dissonance, in the student and make school work overly heavy. Parents strategize in their own way—development of after-school programs and building community schools—to obviate what they perceive to weaknesses in the mainstream approach to literacy and this takes a heavy toll on students' success.

As a matter of fact, mainstream teachers generally fall for meaning-based literacy instruction, while Chinese parents take a dim view of this mode, emphasizing a literacy geared towards skills and phonics. Li argues that the mainstream teachers' approach to literacy is nothing short of Eurocentric and fails to incorporate the worldviews of the Chinese students. Li advocates for an integration of different modes of literacy instruction as meaning-based and skills-based approaches to literacy should never be seen in exclusive terms, but rather as working categories, so interconnected.

In Chapter 7, "Why are the Spanish Speakers in the Back of the Room in a Dual Immersion Setting?" Marisol Ruiz taps into the power of reader's theater as a tool that can serve critical literacy as it can make them autonomous thinkers and productive members of society. With the advent of No Child Left Behind, Reading First has been touted as the single best method for teaching reading with its overemphasis on phonics, fluency, phonemic awareness, vocabulary, and comprehension. Missing in the picture is an attempt to help students read the word in order to read the world (Freire, 2002). Ruiz staunchly advocates for a literacy engagement model because of its ability to engage youth without a fight.

In Chapter 8, "Teaching in the Face of Race: An Autoethnological Theoretical Reflection," Barrel Gueye and Cathie Lalonde analyze their own teaching practices, anchoring their views on their racial subjectivities to unearth the role played by race in classroom dynamics in a higher education setting. The former is Black and African and the latter, White and American.

In this chapter, Gueye and Lalonde use race as a variable in the rapport that is built in classes where teachers engage critical issues around continuous conversations between school and society. Both authors agree that race becomes a factor in sustaining students' interests. They swiftly remark upon the fact that race is not the sole factor, though.

Specifically, when one professor, a Black woman who grew up in Africa, analyzes racial issues, race is seen as "her thing," her area of interest, whereas when the other professor, a White woman originally from the U.S., analyzes these same issues, her students talk about her "passion" for the material, not her race. Not only is race an empty signifier implicated in these different students' responses, but language also plays a part. This chapter raises the complications of the pedagogy of empowerment, problems that arise from teaching being coded historically as powerful or subaltern. This chapter is a conversation starter regarding critical pedagogy, as well as about racial and gender issues as they pertain to teacher identity formation in teacher education programs.

REFERENCES

Freire, P. (2002). *Teachers as cultural workers: Letters to those who dare teach.* Boulder, CO: Westview

Lee, S. (2005). *Up against whiteness: Race, school, and immigrant youth.* New York, NY: Teachers College Press.

Nieto, S. (1992). *Affirming diversity: Sociopolitical   context of multicultural education.* New York, NY: Longman.

Ogbu, J. (1988). *Minority education and caste: The American system in cross-cultural perspectives.* New York, NY: Academic Press.

Ogbu, J., & Simons, D. H. (1998). Voluntary and involuntary minorities: A cultural-ecological theory of school performance with some implications for education. *Anthropology Quarterly, 29*(2), 155–188.

Paré, F. (2004). *La distance habitée.* Ottawa, Ontario: Le Nordir.

Some, T. H. (2012). The invisibility of a visible minority: Where are the African students on the USA campuses? In O. B. Lawuyi & C. Ukpokolo (Eds.), *Space, transformation and representation: Reflections on university culture* (pp. 83–111). Glassboro, NJ: Goldline & Jacobs.

Suarez-Orozco, M. (1987. Becoming somebody: Central American immigrants in U.S. inner-city schools. *Anthropology and Education Quarterly, 18,* 287–298.

Suárez-Orozco, C., & Suárez- Orozco, M. (2002). *Children of immigration.* Cambridge, MA: Harvard University Press.

PART I

IMMIGRANTS, EDUCATION, AND XENOPHOBIA

CHAPTER 1

IN SEARCH OF
A PLACE CALLED HOME

The Linguistic, Cultural, and
Socioeconomic Dislocations of
Immigrants and Transnationals of Color

Pierre Orelus

The narrative of leaving home produces too many homes and hence no Home, too many places in which memories attach themselves through the carving out of inhabitable space, and hence no place that memory can allow the past to reach the present (in which I could declare itself as having come home).

—Sarah Ahmed (2000, p. 78)

Tracing the patterns that connect helps us see that memory is as much social as personal, shaped by the contexts that elicit and give it meaning (Apfelbaum, 2000; Griffin, 2004). The social function of memory is evident in official representations and interpretations of the past (historical memory) that preserve what is to be memorialized and celebrated, and by omission, what is to be ignored and trivialized, thus privileging some stories over others.

—Lee Anne Bell (2010, p. 46)

Immigration and Schooling: Redefining the 21st Century America, pp. 3–24
Copyright © 2015 by Information Age Publishing

First and foremost, writing about immigration and transnationalism requires one to "go back to the source" (Cabral, 1973) in order to reconstruct personal and social memories of one's native land, particularly from childhood or adolescence. This must be done before talking about the Western land to which one is voluntarily or forcibly moved. It is vitally important that one recreates memories of the place that used to be called "back home." As Lee Ann Bell (2010) eloquently puts it, "As a bridge between past and present, social memory shapes identity, informs our interpretations of events, fuels grievances and claims on the present, and suggests what we might imagine for the future" (p. 47). However, for personal and political reasons, some immigrant and transnational subjects may feel that they do not have any place they call "back home," or they might feel that they have multiple homes. Hence, the question becomes: What is home? It is often argued that home is or can be what one wants it to be. It is also widely believed that home does not have to be the country where one was born and where one grew up. Nor does it have to be the country one is forced to move to due to wars, ethnic and intercommunity conflicts, political persecutions, divorces, separation, or other reasons. Finally, it is often said that home does not have to be where one's family and children live, although all of these places can be or feel like home to many people. Situating this question in a transnational context, it is worth further asking: What is home, or what may feel like home to transnational subjects of color living in Western lands? This is the crucial question upon which this chapter seeks to shed light.

The longer immigrant and transnational subjects stay in an adopted country, the harder and more complicated it becomes for many of them to feel that their native land looks like home (Portes & Rumbaut, 2001). Years after immigrant and transnational subjects leave behind their native land to move to and settle to in a "foreign" country, they sometimes feel detached from socioeconomic, cultural, and political realities that once shaped their subjectivity as well as their material conditions when they were living there (Portes & Rumbaut, 2001). In other words, these realities may feel like episodes in their lives or distant memories, which they may not be able to fully reconstruct and relive.

Nonetheless, some immigrants and transnationals may have done things with family members and friends when they first arrived in the West, but experience some difficulty remembering them. This does not mean, however, that they are losing the strong sense of family and communal roots that bind them to family and relatives. One's memory is selective and often preoccupied by different social, racial, or political phenomena that overshadow others. In a moving introduction to his book *Race, Whiteness, and Education*, Zeus Leonardo (2009) narrates a similar experience he had at a family gathering. It is worth quoting Leonardo at length given the relevance of his narrative to this book. Leonardo stated:

> Recently, I attended a family gathering and became reacquainted with cousins whom I have not seen since the late 1970s. Thirty years have passed and like me, these "innocent boys" have grown into men with their own families, careers, and immigrant stories of the United States. During the luncheon, where I gorged myself on lumpia, adobo, and pancit, one male cousin recalled how he and I fought with other boys. I laughed uncomfortably, struggling to recall the scenes from my childhood without clear referents. My cousin assumed that I knew exactly to what he was referring. However, I did not recall engaging in too many fights, let alone with my cousin in two. But it was a reunion and I went along with his "fond" remembrance; I wanted to connect. As he continued his story, he filled it in with details in particular, an altercation with Mexican boys in a Southern California park. It was at this moment that I remembered with precision the scene from childhood, and the flood of memories came from the fight that should have been insignificant. He considered it a bonding moment, something he and I shared as young boys, a masculine story no doubt. Of the several memories he could have relived with me, he considered this one worth remembering three decades later. I was amazed that he recalled a memory that I had also thought about for more than thirty years, one of my clearest introductions to race relations in a U.S. context. It was obviously meaningful to both of us, but perhaps for different reasons. My cousin did not know that I had been trying to make sense of that moment for some time now and it was not the appropriate occasion to seize the opportunity and analyze its racial significance. But this is precisely what I had been doing these many years, sometimes with my students, spouse, or friends, although this is the first time I have written about it. After this brief return to my earliest memories of the USA, my relatives and I continued with the reunion and enjoyed the rest of the afternoon under overcast skies in the Bay Area. (p. 1)

Unlike Leonardo, some immigrants and transnationals may not want to reconstruct their childhood, adolescent, or adult memories from their native or new land because of traumatic experiences they may have had while living there. Traumatic experiences are so painful that one might not want to think about them, let alone reflect on them. Therefore, for many immigrants and transnationals, a temporary solution until these traumas are treated properly might be to block or repress parts of their memories, where images of these traumas are stored. However, this raises several questions that are worth considering: (1) How can one call one's native land home when one doesn't want to remember experiences that happened while living there? (2) Can one call a country or a place home when one's closest family members do not live in that country or place anymore? (3) Can one call a place home when one is no longer welcome, or does not feel welcomed there? (4) Can one call a place home when one doesn't remember, or barely knows who lives there? (6) Should one call a country or a place home when one is treated as merely a visitor when one returns there? Finally, (7) can one call a place or a country home when one is perceived and treated as the "other" and is not allowed to vote because one is a naturalized citizen in a different country?

As these questions suggest, the notion of home is very complex. Feeling at home may be possible for some even under extreme circumstances. For example, being confined in a refugee camp in one's own land, or in foreign land, as a result of political persecutions, wars, intercommunity conflicts, or abject poverty might feel like home to some people. Depending on one's spiritual and philosophical belief, one might make this refugee camp one's home, albeit temporarily. Moreover, sometimes prisons become home for inmates who have been forcibly kept there for a long period of time, despite the horrendous social and psychological conditions they might find themselves in. But how long can feeling at home in these places last under such uncomfortable and inhumane conditions? However ironic and odd this idea may sound to some, feeling at home in such places can stem from one's spiritual or emotional outlook on life.

What one normally calls home is the place where one goes to after long hours of labor, be it physical or intellectual, to rest, unwind, sleep, read, write, and, more importantly, spend time and socialize with loved ones. It can also be a place where one feels comfortable crying and laughing aloud—that is, a place where one feels one can express these emotions without fear of being judged by others. Moreover, home is usually a place where one expresses love for loved ones, raises children, and takes care of one's parents, grandparents, and other family members. Furthermore, what one typically calls home is a place where one goes every year for a family reunion. In brief, home, as so defined, is a place where one usually feels safe psychologically, spiritually, and physically.

On the other hand, the place that has been socially and historically constructed as home sometimes does not feel like home to many people for various reasons. In fact, this place can feel like hell, a place where ghosts live, a place where one may fear psychological, sexual, or physical threats. This place at times brings back painful memories and consequently pushes one to run away from it. Moreover, sometimes living in the type of place that one typically calls home can actually feel worse than feeling homeless. What is worse than feeling homeless in one's home, feeling out of place in one's own home? Hence, it is worth posing once again the question that was posed at the outset of the chapter: What is home?

Searching and finding a place called home is one of the most terrific challenges that many immigrants and transnational subjects often face, as many of them might feel as if they are in exile. Perhaps for many, finding a place that feels like home would remain an unresolved dilemma for decades. Many immigrants and transnational subjects of color were forced to leave their native lands alone or with family members to move to Western lands when they were kids or in the earliest stage of their teenage years (Portes &Rumbaut, 2001). For many of these transnational subjects of color, the phrase "back home" might not trigger strong feelings in them after residing for many years in their adopted country. In other words, they might not feel in their hearts and souls what their parents, grandparents, or other siblings feel when they use or hear the phrase "back home." Though many may have access to and consume what is often called ethnic food, and listen and dance to "music from back home," this experience often does not mean the same thing to them as it means to their parents and grandparents (Portes & Rumbaut, 2001).

Sometimes, many immigrants and transnational subjects of color who move to Western lands while they were very young voluntarily immerse or are forced to immerse themselves in the mainstream culture of the adopted country. Many feel they have to do so, or else they would run the risk of being perceived and treated as an outcast. However, in the process of immersing in the mainstream culture, many lose their native tongue and become somewhat detached from their native culture as they embrace the dominant culture and language (Portes &Rumbaut, 2001). Furthermore, many transnational subjects of color, including academics, who are willingly or forcibly integrated in the mainstream culture simultaneously experience some level of isolation from their academic world and from their community, family members, and friends who may resist being fully integrated in this culture, or who may not be able to do so because of factors such as age and language barriers. In the academic world, they are often treated as minoritized others while in their own community; they might be perceived and treated as outcasts because of social class differences and others. As Leonardo eloquently put it,

> As much as we would like to romanticize our communities, it is also a fact of the matter that we no longer fit into its general population and feel painfully our difference from our families and friends who may not share our educational experience. We cannot return there either, at least not without a great sense of nostalgia. We are that group of intellectuals that Said calls "exiles." Like Freire and Faundez, Said considers the exilic condition a productive (not a synonym for positive) and tensioned experience that is full of knowledge. Never feeling quite entitled to be at home in the academy and having left their communities, they do not belong in either space. Too much of color for the academy and too educated for their communities, scholars of color experience a twoness that they struggle to resolve. They understand the offerings of the academy and therefore share in its mission. They bring with them their lived histories and want only to be allowed to be both an academic and a person of color. The academy perceives them as a qualified

former as it reduces them to the latter. The intellectual of color is in exile, some chosen, to some measure imposed. (Leonardo, 2011, p. 34)

As Leonardo's argument illuminates, many transnational subjects of color sometimes feel like outsiders among their immediate and extended family members because their lifestyle, behavior, and view of both their native land and the Western land clash with that of their parents, grandparents, and siblings. For transnational subjects of color, is it worth paying such a heavy price for immersing in the dominant culture, which, at a deeper level, might not ever fully accept them because of their country of origin and their racial, cultural, linguistic, social class, and religious backgrounds?

Ironically, many immigrants and transnational subjects of color sometimes feel that the "little world" they construct within the dominant world feels more like home to them than the native land where they were born and partially grew up. This is the dilemma that many immigrants and transnational subjects have yet to resolve. I use the word "dilemma" because the dominant culture often doesn't allow a place for those who have been constructed as minorities, or minoritized others, yet many immigrant and transnational subjects of color feel the desire or feel coerced to fit into the dominant culture. The code of the dominant culture is controlled by people of European descent, who often look at postcolonial and transnational subjects of color as the "other," "inferior," "uncivilized," "barbarous," or as "aliens."

In the eyes of those who have invented, controlled, and dictated the codes of the dominant culture (Delpit, 1996), immigrant and transnational subjects of color are not full human beings like them. Therefore, they can't be granted the privilege of being fully integrated in the dominant culture, which has been constructed and destined for the "civilized" and those of the so-called greater and superior human race (Bhabha, 1994). Immigrant and transnational subjects of color have been placed at the margins of the dominant culture for many generations because of the widespread fear that their "barbarous culture" and lifestyle would pollute all the characteristics of their European-based culture. Two former U.S. presidential candidates, Pat Buchanan and Mitt Romney, who are fierce anti-immigrant advocates, are among the U.S. pundits who have circulated this type of fear through the mainstream media. These pundits have often made xenophobic statements about immigrants from Mexico and other so-called Third World countries. Buchanan (2004), for example, stated:

And the Mexican people? Half the 100 million are still mired in poverty. Tens of millions are unemployed or underemployed. Because of devaluations, real wages are below what they were in 1993. Thus the great migration north continues. Some 1.5 million are apprehended every year on our southern border breaking into the United States. Of the perhaps 500,000 who make it, one-third head for Mexifornia where their claims on Medicaid, schools, courts, prisons, and welfare have tipped the Golden State toward bankruptcy and induced millions of native-born Americans to flee in the great exodus to Nevada, Idaho, Arizona, and Colorado. Ten years after NAFTA, Mexico's leading export to America is still—Mexicans. America is becoming Mexamerica. (p. 166)

It is worth pointing out, however, that throughout history, some limited and controlled space has been granted to those who have proven to be or are perceived to be less threatening minoritized groups; this is seen as a way to promote racial diversity. Nonetheless, those who have dictated the rules of the game of the dominant culture are usually the same group of people who have controlled the socioeconomic and political structures of the country, whether it is in the United States or in European countries. For example, Western pundits, including E. D. Hirsch (1987), Allan Bloom (1989), and Diane Ravitch (1990) have criticized parents and teachers for not encouraging their minoritized children and students to assimilate into and embrace what Hirsch (1987) called the "common culture."

Along with common culture, Hirsch (1987) talks about core knowledge, which he believes every student in the U.S. school system should be able to access. For more than 20 years, Hirsch has strongly advocated a common culture and core knowledge that is European-based and completely detached from the cultural, sociohistorical, and political realities of minoritized subjects such as transnational and postcolonial subjects of color as well as other marginalized groups. For these marginalized groups, a European-based curriculum might revive in their memory history of colonialism—that is, a history of pillage, exploitation, violence, and murder of colonized people, including Native Americans and African Americans. Therefore, it is doubtful that this common culture and core knowledge can be meaningful to these marginalized groups. How can they relate to this core knowledge when it reminds them of the mistreatment and enslavement of their parents, grandparents, and ancestors? Kamberelis and Dimitriadis (2005) explain what Hirsch's cultural framework entails, and they challenge it in the following terms:

> The cultural knowledge that Hirsch has in mind is presumed to be "common culture" and not elite culture, even though it derives primarily from canonical works within a white, European-American, middle- to upper-class, heterosexist tradition. Within a cultural literacy framework, it is assumed that there is a neutral canon of key cultural knowledge that all students should know. It is also assumed this body of knowledge exists outside of the individual subject and can be learned, usually through direct instruction and study. This neutral body of knowledge is transmitted to individual subjects through the neutral medium of Standard English. Finally, Hirsch asserts that

if students lack a particular and prescribed set of cultural knowledge, then they will be unable to read and write adequately or function productively in society. (p. 30)

While one should not be ethnocentric, that is, close-minded with regard to other cultures and to the history of other people, one should never be forced to embrace a common culture that might be alienating to one's spirit, soul, and mind. To paraphrase Linda Smith (1999), one should never be forced to embrace a European-based culture and core knowledge at the expense of one's indigenous culture and knowledge. Immigrant and transnational subjects of color do assimilate into dominant Western culture. Unfortunately, such assimilation often leads to their marginalization. As Aviva Chomsky (2007) puts it, "It's not a lack of assimilation that keeps them marginalized—it's assimilation itself" (p. 106). Chomsky goes on to say,

The picture is clear. Immigrants of color do assimilate into U.S. society, but, in contrast to white immigrants, for people of color assimilation means downward mobility. Assimilation means learning the racial order of the United States, and for people of color it means joining the lower ranks of that racial order. The association often made between assimilation and upward mobility is based on the experience of white immigrants. For immigrants of color, the trajectory of assimilation is a very different one. (p. 108)

One should have the opportunity to explore and understand the culture and core knowledge of any group, including the dominant group, but this should not be done at the expense of one's human dignity and cultural heritage.

Hence, in the case of immigrant and transnational subjects of color, further questions should be asked: (1) How can immigrant and transnational subjects of color feel at home while being willingly or forcibly immersed in this common culture? (2) How can they be apprenticed into such culture when they feel alienated from it spiritually, psychologically, culturally? (3) How can transnational and postcolonial subjects of color use that core knowledge, for which Hirsch (1987) has advocated, and still feel at home? (4) Can immigrant and transnational subjects of color and other disenfranchised groups such as African Americans, Native Americans, Latino/as, Arabs, and Asians feel a sense of community within this common culture? To put it simply, can these marginalized subjects feel they are part of a community while being immersed in the common culture?

One's culture is embedded in a community. Cultural artifacts such as clothes, food, dance, music, folklore, language, folktales, and beliefs constitute integral parts of one's community. Without these artifacts, a community simply does not exist. Therefore, one feels part of a community when one can share some of these cultural characteristics. Likewise, one feels at home within a culture when one's community shapes the culture. In other words, home, culture, and community are interconnected.

As a prime example, many immigrant and transnational subjects of color feel at home when they go back to their native land to visit family members, friends, and neighbors because they enjoy the sense of community and culture there: the common language, the food or the smell of the food, the music, the common and cultural inside jokes that don't require translation or explanation, the sense of bonding with others, the feeling of belonging to something bigger and more profound than oneself. In short, it is the sense of community. As these examples illustrate, home is intrinsically linked to community.

HOME AND COMMUNITY

At the outset, I want to argue that there cannot be home without a community. In other words, feeling at home means feeling part of a community. Community in this context is defined as a place where people support each other and care for one another, and where there is an open and honest communication between members of that community, and where conflicts of any kind are resolved through genuine dialogue by members of the community. Conflicts are not resolved with fists, weapons, or various forms of intimidation. It's also a place where one feels safe from hypocrisy, conspiracy, betrayal, vicious forms of jealousy, hatred, physical violence, or "symbolic violence" (Bourdieu, 1990) that is racially, culturally, linguistically, sexually, religiously, class-, and gender-based. This type of community does not have to be created or found in a neighborhood. It can be found anywhere. To paraphrase Benedict Anderson (2006), even if it is not possible to create or be a part of such a community, it can be imagined. Needless to say, it is vitally important that one feels at home situated in the context of a community.

As noted earlier, for many immigrants and transnational subjects of color, feeling part of a community usually happens when they go back home or when they are among people who share their cultural heritage, and racial, linguistic, and religious backgrounds. This sense of community might not exist for many in the Western mainstream and dominant culture that often pushes them to racial, linguistic, and religious margins. This sense of rejection from Western dominant culture explains why many transnational and postcolonial subjects of color feel the natural inclination and desire to reach out to people whom they feel are part of their community. Furthermore, the sense of Western marginalization they experience challenges many to look for a community to which they feel they belong.

While some move to states where they can find and mingle with people with whom they share cultural, linguistic, historical, and religious bonds, others go back home to spend holidays with family and friends, for doing so may be the only way they can feel at home and be part of a community.

Sadly, however, there are some transnational subjects of color who do not feel at home within the community that they should be able to call their own. One may feel rejected by one's community, due to a lack of tolerance toward, for example, members of the community who have a different lifestyle or sexual orientation from what is commonly accepted and normalized within that community (Anzaldúa, 2007). There may be a lack of tolerance for ideological and religious differences or outlooks on life. Moreover, those who are westernized or are embracing and valuing the dominant Western lifestyle might not feel welcome within certain communities that scorn this lifestyle. Finally, people may not feel welcome within their own community if, through Western acculturation and full immersion, they lose their first language and are not familiar with the cultural norms that bind a community together (Portes & Rumbaut, 2001).

Certain factors may make one feel unwelcomed by people within a community. Sometimes, through body language, or in other ways, insensitive and intolerant members of a community may remind transnational subjects of color that they are not integral members of that community because of their inability to speak the language spoken in that community, or because of the way they dress or behave, or simply because of their inability to relate to other members of the community.

Transnational subjects of color who move to Western lands when they are very young often experience this type of isolation within their community. What often happens is that over the years, these transnational subjects lose their native language and consequently become somewhat detached from the community of which they used to be a part. The rituals, folklore, and other cultural artifacts that shape this community become somewhat foreign to them. Because these cultural elements are vital to the survival of a community and because these groups of transnational and postcolonial subjects of color are no longer familiar with or fully embrace these elements, many feel alienated from a community that was once theirs.

Within the Western culture that they embrace, they might also feel alienated for the reasons mentioned earlier. Therefore, this category of transnational subjects of color end up being doubly marginalized and isolated; that is, they do not feel at home either within their own community or the community they either voluntarily or were forced to embrace. So the questions become: What is home, or what can possibly be or feel like home for them? Furthermore, what is the community to which they feel or might feel they belong?

For this specific group of immigrant and transnational subjects of color, a home or a community may be something abstract and imaginary, or something they feel in their heart—that is, something they can only imagine, dream of, sometimes crave and wish for, but not something they can experience and enjoy. This may explain why many transnational subjects of color often claim that they do not have any home, or that they have multiple homes, even though these types of homes may be elusive. This situation may apply to immigrant and transnational subjects of color who have been living in Western lands for a decade or more and who go back home once in a while to visit family members, friends, and neighbors. These immigrant and transnational subjects of color may not be fully accepted in their community back home, for other members of that community who never left their native lands might look at them as evasive members or strangers. This may be even truer for those who left behind their community to immigrate to Western lands when they were kids or teenagers. These transnational subjects of color might feel caught between the West and their countries of origin, but not part of either. When going "back home," they are often treated as visitors or, worse yet, as strangers, while in their host Western country many are perceived and treated as "invaders," "foreigners," or simply as "dirty immigrants" of color.

In terms of home, community, and culture, how does a transnational subject of color find his or her sense of belonging? Is it with the culture once shared with parents, grandparents, and siblings? Or is it the dominant culture that many are forced to embrace and yet alienates them? Perhaps a third cultural and communal space can be created for transnational subjects of color. If so, how would they go about creating that space and whom should they include? If the created community only includes people who have been isolated from their own community and culture as well as the Western dominant culture and community, this third community only succeeds in reproducing the same alienation that victimized those who were seeking community. Obviously, this topic raises more questions than answers. However, what is becoming more evident every day is that many transnational subjects who feel isolated by both their own community and the mainstream and dominant culture end up making poor choices that are sometimes hazardous to their lives and impact society in negative ways. For example, like many other marginalized groups, many transnational youth of color who feel marginalized by society end up being involved in gangs and other unsafe activities.

As Robert Duran (2013) argued in his book, *Gang Life in Two Cities*, for youth of color, the gang becomes their home and community and the gang members become the people they can confide in. The socioeconomic, cultural, and political oppression and isolation they experience in Western society lead many to create their own world where they feel at home. Social upheaval and unrest emerge from these created worlds, as we witnessed in some ghettoized neighborhoods in France in 2005. Among the youth of color who participated in this riot were transnational subjects of color who immigrated to France when they were kids; others were the first generation born to immigrants from Algeria and other African and Caribbean countries.

These immigrant and transnational youths of color took to the streets to burn cars and houses as a sign of protest of the murder of a friend, neighbor, and family member. But the protesters were not born violent. Social marginalization led them to commit these acts of violence and disorder. Like any other marginalized group in society, these transnational youths of color were aware of their longstanding marginalization and the decades of politicians' lies they and their parents and neighbors had been told about their miserable socioeconomic conditions.

Unlike many people in academia, these youths did not have to learn about socioeconomic and political marginalization from books. They experienced it in their dilapidated neighborhoods every day, while politicians made false and empty promises in televised speeches. For the youths, there was a clear disconnect between what the politicians said on TV, what they learned from their school textbooks about their socioeconomic and political conditions, and what happened in their neighborhoods and their lives. One does not have to be a genius to understand the root causes of their violent revolt against the status quo, socioeconomic inequality, and political and cultural isolation. Just a month or two spent living in their poor neighborhoods and observing the horrendous socioeconomic conditions in which they lived would help most people understand the underlying reasons that led many to take to the streets in protest. Unless actions are taken to remedy socioeconomic inequality and to eradicate racial, ethnic, cultural, and linguistic oppression faced by many transnational subjects of color, we are likely to witness similar riots in other Western imperialist countries such as the United States and United Kingdom.

As noted earlier, most, if not all, immigrant and transnational subjects of color move to the West in search for a better life for themselves and their family. Unlike the mainstream media and dominant discourse that have portrayed many of them as deviant, violent, and lazy people, many transnational subjects of color would prefer to stay in their native lands if they were not destroyed economically and politically by Western socioeconomic and political policies as well as the actions of their corrupt leaders. Therefore, there is no reason to believe that transnational subjects of color migrate to Western lands to cause trouble or to be involved in gang activities and riots.

The root cause of many violent actions committed by transnational subjects of color lies in a system where racism, linguicism, xenophobia, sexism, and classism push underserved youths to the margins. While their violent actions should not be justified, it can be understood. Unless we, as a society, make the effort to understand and eradicate the root causes that have led many transnational youth of color to engage in violent and unsafe activities, we will continue to witness social upheaval and unrest rising from socially, economically, and politically marginalized places.

It must be noted that not all immigrant and transnational subjects of color embark on violent actions in response to their socioeconomic, political, cultural, and linguistic marginalization. A significant number have sought church or religious organizations as their escape or as their alternative home. This group of transnational subjects often joins culturally and ethnically diverse churches where their language is spoken and their culture is valued. Within these churches, they create their own community and feel at home. These churches become for them a place where they find comfort and reassurance that they are somebody, rather than second-class citizens and aliens who are invading western lands.

Similarly, there are transnational and postcolonial subjects of color, such as Muslims, who have found ways to create their own community where they profess their religious beliefs. For many, the religious community they create may be the source of inspiration and moral strength to continue fighting xenophobia and racial oppression in the larger society. Unfortunately, mosques have been under state and federal surveillance, especially since the September 11th terrorist attack. Since this tragedy, Arabs or, for that matter, anyone who looks Arab, has been racially profiled almost everywhere: at school, at the airport, at work, on the street, and in other settings.

In his book, *How Does It Feel to Be a Problem*, Moustafa Bayoumi (2008) draws on the narratives of many young Arabs and Muslims to demonstrate how they have been targeted and marginalized for being Muslims and Arabs. Muslims, whether they are Arab or not, have been victims of many forms of symbolic violence (Bourdieu, 1990, 1991). Mosques have been sabotaged and dishonored. For example, in 2010, an Islamic center in Springfield, Massachusetts, was attacked by a group of Islamophobic individuals who threw rotten fruit, wrote threatening graffiti on the wall of the mosque, and made threatening phone calls to the Muslim leaders of the center (Constantine, 2010). As columnist Sandra Constantine reports:

> Local Muslims say hostilities against them and their religion have flared up in recent weeks in the wake of the heated controversies about a proposed mosque near Ground Zero, the threatened burning of the Quran and the 9/11 anniversary. Hostilities include graffiti on signs, a nasty telephone message and apples thrown at midnight at the home of the imam of the mosque on Amostown Road, according to Muslim leaders. Graffiti on signs at and leading to the mosque has included the image of a devil, they said. A tele-

phone message left at the mosque and replayed for a reporter accused its
members of raising money to kill women and children. (p. 1)

Moreover, a pastor in Florida named Terry Jones threatened to burn
the Quran on the ninth anniversary of September 11th in protest of the
proposed mosque near Ground Zero. After being challenged and discour-
aged by key political figures such as U.S. Secretary of State Hillary Clinton
and Secretary of Defense Robert Gates, Terry Jones opted not to burn the
Quran. However, later in March 2010 he decided to burn the Quran after
all. His action incited much violence and undoubtedly caused psychological and religious damage to many Muslims. These types of symbolic
violence are terrifying to those they target. Other religious groups such as
Catholics or Mormons would feel threatened if the Bible or their places of
worship were attacked in this way.

There is another group of transnational subjects of color who have
explored a nonviolent alternative to their racial marginalization in the West.
This group often returns to their native lands to spend time with family,
neighbors, and friends. They have managed throughout the years to stay
in touch with their roots. They tend to have emigrated at a younger age.

What is refreshing about going back home to visit family and friends is
that one does not have to worry about being discriminated against because
of one's racial, linguistic, and cultural backgrounds. In most cases, transnational subjects of color speak the same language and share a common
cultural heritage with their family, friends, and neighbors back home.
However, they may face serious issues when they return. For example, they
run the risk of being robbed by natives who target them as visitors from the
United States and other western countries.

Furthermore, social class is sometimes an issue. The natives who are of
lower class and in abject poverty might perceive transnational subjects of
color visiting from the West with a different eye. They may see them as
people with economic capital who can rescue them from poverty. Moreover, some transnational subjects of color may feel overwhelmed by family
members and friends who want to take advantage of them financially or
directly ask for an exorbitant sum of money. These are some of the challenges that some transnational subjects of color face, especially those who
are from poor countries and/or poor family backgrounds.

However, while visiting their native lands, they do not have to worry
about major social problems such as racial profiling and discrimination
in the workforce and at school, problems they face daily in Western lands.
Nor are they treated like second-class citizens as they are in the West.
Furthermore, they do not have to constantly worry about their humanity
being insulted by those who feel superior to them. Nor do they have to be
concerned that their blood pressure and blood sugar level might escalate

because of the individual and institutional racism to which they are subjected daily. Moreover, they do not have to worry about being discriminated against because of their foreign accent and "alien" status. Finally, while being with their family members, friends, and neighbors back home, transnational subjects of color are exempt from being unfairly arrested, wrongly convicted, jailed, and wrongly executed, as has happened to many African Americans and Latino/as because of their racial background.

Visiting family, friends, and neighbors back home is usually, if not always, an opportunity for transnational and postcolonial subjects to enjoy and appreciate life free of the excess stress and social problems they face in the West. Although I don't go back to my native land as often as I would like to, when I do, I always feel like a different person in that I don't have to worry about the constant racial harassment and linguistic discrimination that I face in the United States. Like many transnational subjects of color, I am much happier being among people who look at me as a person first and foremost, and not only as Black.

Despite the horrible socioeconomic and political conditions in which Haiti has existed for decades, when I go back there to visit loved ones, I sleep better at night and I do not feel stressed walking on the street, for I do not have to worry about being targeted by the police and individual racist people because I'm Black. Furthermore, when I speak in my native tongue, I don't have to worry about being discriminated against because of accent issues. In addition to the natural foods and organic vegetables and fruits I can enjoy there, I have the privilege of enjoying the company of humble people who value human beings over material things such as cars and money.

The privilege I have as a transnational subject of color is that I have a place to go to when I need to save my sanity and uplift my morale, which have been weakened by racism, linguicism, and other forms of oppression experienced in United States. Often, I feel the strongest desire to escape to Haiti when I feel appalled by racial and linguistic discrimination and other forms of discrimination that marginalized transnational subjects of color have faced in western lands, especially those who have been forced to live in marginalized places called the ghetto because of their racial and social class backgrounds.

However, despite the positive feelings I experience when I return to Haiti, the truth is that I still do not feel completely at home when I am there. The primary reason is that I feel detached from the daily harsh socioeconomic and political realities facing the struggling, poor, working-class people living there. When I go to Haiti, many of my old friends, family members, and neighbors look at me with a different eye, although they still welcome me warmly and with love. In their eyes, I am no longer the little poor boy I used to be. Nor am I the high school and college student who used to live next to them in the "bidonville" (i.e., the ghetto) and who used to walk miles to school, often on an empty stomach. They perceive and treat me differently because in their eyes, I am living in the richest country in the world and they all dream of going there some day.

Even though going back to my native land feels like an escape from the brutality of racism, xenophobia, and linguicism, being there does not completely feel like home because of the reasons just mentioned. In fact, when I go to Haiti, I usually have someone accompany me when going out, because I am afraid of getting lost in certain neighborhoods that I barely recognize. These neighborhoods, which I knew very well as a boy, have become overcrowded and dilapidated. Moreover, my family and friends are afraid I might get robbed or even killed if I walk alone down the streets. How can I feel at home under such circumstances? Finally, is it logical to claim that I am at home in a country whose socioeconomic and political reality I am losing sight of every day?

What is home for me then? Is it the United States? More specifically, is it the project housing in Cambridge, Massachusetts, where I moved to and lived for a year after coming from my native land in the early 1990s? As much as I wanted the project housing in Cambridge to feel like home to me, I could not help but think of my safety every day while living there. The frequent drug trafficking and constant fights among neighbors living next door did not allow me to feel at home in that place; nor did the harassment of the housing personnel who pressured my sister-in-law to move out of her apartment because she allowed me to stay with her illegally, sharing a room with my 2½-year-old niece.

Is it then Arlington, Belchertown, Amherst, or Easthampton, Massachusetts, where I lived over a period of five years and experienced the daily harassment of some White police officers? The constant racial profiling to which I was subject and the sense of isolation that I felt living next to Caucasian neighbors who would ignore me when I greeted them prevented me from feeling at home in my neighborhood. There were times in Easthampton when I did not feel safe in the home I purchased because I became annoyed by and fearful of a police officer who regularly patrolled my street.

It did not matter that my wife and I were graduate students who were striving to do well in school while working multiple part-time jobs to support ourselves. The police officer seemed to be mainly concerned about the only two people of color living on that street. Therefore, he had to keep an eye on us. It did not matter that we were quiet, responsible, and good citizens like most people in our neighborhood. Neither our neighbors nor the police officer tried to get to know us as a young and dynamic couple who were trying to do what is expected of us: go to school, work hard, and build a family.

I did not feel at home at any of these places because of the painful racist experiences I had while living there. Does Las Cruces, New Mexico, the city where I got my first tenure-track faculty position after finishing my doctorate, feel like home to me? New Mexico is called the land of enchantment. As the name suggests, it is a state where people should feel relaxed and happy. In many ways, Las Cruces is the most relaxing place I've ever lived. People seem so tranquil and easy going. Unlike Massachusetts, New Mexico reminds me of my native land. As in some places in Haiti, it's dry and desert-like. The weather is closer to what I was used to when I was living in Haiti than the cold weather in Massachusetts. Furthermore, Las Cruces is more diverse than some cities in Massachusetts where I had lived. Caucasians and Mexican Americans are the majority in Las Cruces. From what I've observed, there are not many Blacks, let alone Haitians or people from the Caribbean.

Although I do not have any problem mingling with people from different races and ethnicities who are not racist, I often feel homesick living in Las Cruces. I wish there were more people of diverse racial and ethnic backgrounds here. My desire to see people of more diverse backgrounds residing in this city is not informed by any ethnocentric view; nor is it informed by any racist tendency or belief. The truth is that I would rather be living in a place where people from different races are mingled. I sometimes feel like a "minority within minorities" (Montero-Sieburth, 2000) living in Las Cruces.

Not only am I among very few Blacks, but I am also one of the very few Caribbean people living in this beautiful city. Culturally and linguistically, I sometimes feel isolated even though I speak Spanish, which is one of the dominant languages spoken here. For these reasons, I do not feel completely at home in Las Cruces despite its beautiful scenery, quietness, and the friendliness of many people, including some of my colleagues whom I sincerely admire. What is home for me? I honestly do not feel that I have one. These unpleasant experiences have made me realize that place fundamentally matters when it comes to one's feeling at home and as part of community. Indeed, place matters.

PLACE MATTERS

Why does place matter? I'll attempt to answer this question in this section. The simplest and most direct answer may be that place matters because the place where one lives is a fundamental indicator of one's social status. Furthermore, place matters because the neighborhood where one lives can be a determining factor in one's overall health and life expectancy. Place is not just a place, as some may assume. There is a history that shapes a place. Places are not innocently conceived, nor do they vaguely come into existence. The construction, protection, maintenance, and survival of a place is economically, socially, and politically motivated. A place is nothing without people inhabiting it or history and culture shaping it. To put it simply, a place in itself is voiceless and innocent. However, as people take over a place, they mold it and make it become something else for either their own individualistic needs at the expense of others or for the overall benefit of a community. It is no accident that people move to certain places for specific reasons.

Many transnational subjects of color have been forced to live in marginalized places due to socioeconomic inequality and racism. These places are often overcrowded with fast-food restaurants, like McDonald's and Burger King, and liquor stores. Fresh vegetables and fruit, which human beings need to consume in order to live a healthy life, are often scarce at the neighborhood supermarkets. Moreover, safe, clean places to exercise or hang out with friends and family are often nonexistent. The places where poor transnational subjects of color are concentrated often lack health clinics or clean, safe water. The air is polluted by industrial chemicals, there is a lack of sanitation and proper sewage and irrigation, and garbage collects on the street. Finally, because of abject poverty and a sense of hopelessness resulting from a chronic form of racism and "savage inequalities" (Kozol, 1992), prostitution and drug trafficking have become common practice in these places.

Consequently, because of their low income, transnational subjects of color living in these marginalized places are left with no other option but to consume what's available at McDonald's and Burger King. Such an unhealthy diet, combined with little opportunity for exercise, is a deadly combination. Conditions such as diabetes and heart disease are avoidable under healthier living conditions, but, in these communities, they lead to what is called "excess death"; that is, early death that could have been avoided but is rampantly increasing in these communities. A high death rate due to alcoholism, drug addiction, drug trafficking, overdoses, and AIDS have become their reality. These early deaths, to paraphrase Kozol (1985), are socially, economically, and politically conditioned. They do not have to occur in the neglected places where transnational subjects of color and other marginalized groups live, but that has been the reality for decades. Racism and social policies are at the root of the horrendous socioeconomic and political conditions that have led to the early death of many transnational subjects of color.

To remedy the horrible racial, socioeconomic, and political conditions to which transnational and postcolonial subjects of color have been subjected, a new racial contract (Mills, 1999) is the sine qua non condition. Such a contract will benefit every sector and member of society, for it will minimize the high rate of gang violence affecting everyone. This type of violence often emerges from neglected and marginalized neighborhoods. To put it simply, a well-thought-out social policy should, first and foremost, aim to eradicate poverty, or at least reduce the level of poverty among marginalized groups in society. As the old saying goes, there can't be peace without justice. The type of justice that is referred to here should not merely be social justice, but also racial, sexual, and economic justice.

Socioeconomic, racial, sexual, and political justice has been hijacked by the wealthy for centuries, especially those who happen to be born in the "right" skin—that is, the skin that symbolizes privileges or access to many unearned opportunities and who have oppressed others to maintain the status quo. Like many marginalized groups such as African Americans, Native Americans, and Latin Americans, many transnational subjects of color who have been living in Western lands for generations have yet to see this type of justice for themselves. They have been victims of racial, socioeconomic, linguistic, and political injustice from the first month or year they set foot on the shore of Western lands such as France, the United States, and United Kingdom. Generations that come after them have also been subject to the same form of social injustice. Their experience complicates and challenges the Western definition of democracy. When referring to democracy in France, the United States, and United Kingdom, one needs to question what kind of democracy it truly is. For whose benefit was this concept invented, and who has benefited from it for centuries?

The painful experiences of many transnational subjects of color also challenge the notion that the United States is, for example, a melting pot. Who is really at the center of the melting pot? Who is at its periphery? And why? These are the fundamental questions that one needs to continue to ask as certain groups of people continue to be racially marginalized because of their country of origin, nationality, race, religion, and social class.

Historically, in the United States of America, the melting-pot discourse has been used as propaganda to cover up racial discrimination and other forms of oppression to which transnational subjects of color and other marginalized groups have been subjected. The phrase "melting pot" is supposed to mean a fusion of different races, ethnicities, nationalities, cultures, and languages. It is commonly used as an umbrella term to describe the fusion of immigrants and other inhabitants living in the United States. On the surface, this sounds like a noble idea, in the sense that people mingle regardless of their cultural, ethnic, linguistic, religious, and social class differences.

However, socioeconomic, racial, and political realities suggest the opposite. Transnational subjects, especially transnational subjects of color, have not been allowed to be part of the "melting pot," usually because of their racial, linguistic, cultural backgrounds and country of origin. In other words, race, nationality, language, sexuality, religion, and social class have prevented many from being fully accepted in the melting pot. Understood from this standpoint, the melting pot is an illusion for many transnational subjects of color.

Specifically, it is an illusion for many who have been forced to live in segregated neighborhoods. Because of institutional racism and xenophobia, many transnationals of color have not been allowed to live in what are called "good neighborhoods"—that is, affluent neighborhoods that are predominantly inhabited by privileged Whites. They have been forced to live at the margins of these "good neighborhoods." Even middle-class transnational subjects of color are sometimes denied housing in neighborhoods designated for wealthy Whites.

In addition to housing segregation, many transnational subjects of color are often isolated in the U.S. school system. For example, while in college, many feel they have to create their own groups or student organizations, as they often feel marginalized by dominant groups on campus. They are often perceived and treated as "foreigner" or the "other" by those from the dominant groups, usually composed of privileged, conservative Whites.

The noble idea behind the melting-pot propaganda can't become a reality for transnational subjects of color as long as these forms of segregation persist. Nor can transnational subjects of color ever feel at home and part of a melting pot if certain racial and ethic groups dominate and dictate the terms of such a pot. Those who have been given the privilege of being situated at the center of the melting pot by virtue of their race and social class can and should feel they are part of it. However, transnational and postcolonial subjects of color, especially those who are poor, have been pushed to the margins. They are not part of the melting pot.

The melting pot will feel like home for every transnational and non-transnational when, we as a society, make the necessary effort to fight against and eradicate institutional racism, xenophobia, homophobia, linguicism, classism, and sexism. Moreover, the melting-pot propaganda that has been circulated in the mainstream media and in canonical texts will become a reality for everyone living in this land of opportunity if and only if we, as a people, unite and strive to radically change the structure of the socioeconomic and political system of this country. The mere fact that we now have the son of a transnational African as the first Black president in the most powerful country in the West does not mean things will fundamentally improve for transnational subjects of color.

This system has been set up to benefit mainly people of European descent, especially wealthy, heterosexual, and able-bodied White males. Therefore, if transnational subjects of color and other marginalized groups want to disrupt and transgress the terms of the melting pot, first and foremost, they need to be united and fight against two common and major enemies: institutional racism and xenophobia. Unless they do so, the advent of the true melting pot will remain a mere illusion. Those in power have been the ones deciding who enters the melting and who does not. Therefore, unless we stand up, fight for our rights, and demand to be included in it, we will continue to be pushed to the margins.

The names and migration stories of many transnational subjects of color have been used by those in power to socially and historically construct the so-called melting pot. However, transnationals have not been the main beneficiaries of this pot. It is time transnational subjects of color and other marginalized groups strived to make the melting pot feel like home to all of them, for they are pillars of this country. In my view, the United States would not exist without the hard work of many transnational subjects of color who were dislocated from their native lands due to the corruption of leaders of their countries of origin, Western countries' foreign policy, and unfair trade agreements such as NAFTA, which led, for instance, to the destruction of the Mexican economy (Chomsky, 2011).

The sacrifice many transnational subjects of color made fighting here and abroad for the hegemonic economic and geopolitical interests of the United States and other imperialist countries should not be in vain. In other words, they should fully feel at home in the United States and other Western countries such as the United Kingdom and France, because many of their family members have lost their lives in wars defending the interests of these countries. Equally important, all transnational subjects deserve to be part of their community here and back home, regardless of their country of origin or cultural, linguistic, religious, sexual, and social-class backgrounds, because "back home" is where their umbilical cords were buried and where their roots are. To feel isolated by one's own community, either here or back home, is nothing but social injustice.

REFERENCES

{ref}Ahmed, S. (2000). *Strange encounters: Embodied others in post-coloniality.* New York, NY: Routledge.

Anderson, B. (2006). *Imagined communities: Reflections on the origin and spread of nationalism.* London, England: Verso.

Anzaldúa, G. (2007). *Borderlands/La frontera: The new mestiza* (3rd ed.). San Francisco, CA: Aunt Lute Books.

Bayoumi, M. (2008). *How does it feel to be a problem? Being young and Arab in America.* New York, NY: Penguin Press.

Bell, L. A. (2010). *Storytelling for social justice: Connecting narrative and the arts in antiracist teaching.* New York, NY: Routledge.

Bhabha, H. (1994). *The location of culture.* London, England: Routledge.

Bloom, A. (1989). *The closing of the American mind.* New York, NY: Simon & Schuster.

Bourdieu, P. (1990). *The logic of practice* (R. Nice, Trans.). Stanford, CA: Stanford University Press.

Bourdieu, P. (1991*). Language and symbolic power* (G. Raymond & M. Adamso, Trans.). Cambridge, England: Polity.

Buchanan, P. (2004). *Where the right went wrong: How neoconservatives subverted the Reagan revolution and hijacked the Bush presidency.* New York, NY: Thomas Dunne Books.

Cabral, A. (1973). *Return to the source: Selected speeches by Amílcar Cabral.* New York, NY: Monthly Review Press.

Chomsky, A. (2007). *They take our jobs: And 20 other myths about immigration.* Boston, MA: Beacon Press.

Chomsky, N. (2011). *Profits over people: Neoliberalism and global order* (2nd edition). New York, NY: Seven Stories Press.

Constantine, S. (2010, September 10). Western Massachusetts Muslims say hostilities against them flaring up. *The Republican.* Retrieved from http://www.masslive.com/news/index.ssf/2010/09/western_massachusetts_muslims_1.html.

Delpit, L. (1996). The silenced dialogue: Power and pedagogy in educating other people's children. *Harvard Educational Review,* 280–298.

Duran, R. (2013). *Gang life in two cities: An insider's journey.* New York, NY: Columbia University Press.

Hirsch, E. D., Jr. (1987). *Cultural literacy: What every American needs to know.* New York, NY: Vintage.

Kamberelis, G., & Dimitriadis, G. (2005). *Qualitative inquiry: Approaches to language and literary research.* New York, NY: Teachers College.

Kozol, J. (1985). *Death at an early age.* New York, NY: Plume.

Kozol, J. (1992). *Savage inequalities: Children in America's schools.* New York, NY: Crown.

Leonardo, Z. (2009). *Race, whiteness, and education.* New York, NY: Routledge.

Leonardo, Z. (2011). Unmasking White supremacy and racism: A conversation with Zeus Leonardo. In P. Orelus (Ed.), *Rethinking race, class, language, and gender: A dialogue with Noam Chomsky and other leading scholars* (pp. 31–51). Lanham, MD: Rowman & Littlefield.

Mills, C. (1999). *The racial contract.* Ithaca, NY: Cornell University Press.

Montero-Sieburth, M. (2000). The use of cultural resilience in overcoming contradictory encounters in academia: A personal narrative. In E. H. Trueba & L. Bartolome (Eds.), *Immigrant voices: In search of educational equity* (pp. 218–245). Lanham, MD: Rowman & Littlefield.

Portes, A., & Rumbaut, R. (2001). *Legacies: The story of the immigrant second generation.* Berkeley, CA: University of California.

Ravitch, D. (1990). Diversity and democracy: Multicultural education in America. *American Educator, 14*(1), 16–20, 46–68.

Smith, L. T. (1999). *Decolonizing methodologies: Research and indigenous people.* London, England: Zed Books.

CHAPTER 2

EDUCATION OF IMMIGRANTS' CHILDREN[1]

A Review of Four Decades of Empirical Research in the United States 1965–2011[2]

Yan Z. Ciupak

In 2011, about one out every four children ages 0–17 come from an immigrant family, representing a doubling of this population from 1990.[3] The shift of American demography in the U.S. has sparked widespread discussions on issues related to immigrants. There is wide concern and interest over issues such as immigrants' children's adaptation to the society and their school performance, and what this means to the future of American society. This chapter reviews four decades of empirical research in the United States relevant to education of immigrants' descendents in order to provide an overview of the research results for policymakers, scholars, educators, and others working closely with children of immigrants.

Much of the educational research since 1960 focuses on the ways in which schools privilege some groups of children while simultaneously marginalizing others. Groups exhibit differential dropout rates (Rumberger, 1983, 1995; Rumberger & Thomas, 2000), attend different schools (Orfield,

Immigration and Schooling: Redefining the 21st Century America, pp. 25–37
Copyright © 2015 by Information Age Publishing

1978, 1996; Fuller, Elmore, & Orfield, 1996: Orfield & Lee, 2004) and are exposed to differential knowledge in terms of curriculum-in-use. Knowledge tends to have a social class content, thus embodying the interests and history of the privileged and the powerful. While such work has been articulate in many respects, much of it tends to construe difference along a narrowly constructed Black–White dichotomy. In other words, much contemporary work on schooling, when it takes into account difference among students in schools, focuses on African American and Caucasian students rather than recognize the complexity of the American landscape. In recent years, research has expanded so as to recognize growing heterogeneity within the "Black" and "White" communities as well as a wide range of additional communities, many of them Latino or Asian, whose children are now in American schools.

While diversity certainly did not begin in the late 20th century (when research in the field on such topics grew), current unprecedented diversity in United States schools has spawned a set of research questions related to children and families who are relatively new to American schools such as Haitians (Laguerre, 1997; Stepick, 1998), Dominicans (Pessar, 1997), Africans and Caribbeans of varying nationality (Rong & Brown, 2001, 2002), Vietnamese (Bankston & Zhou, 1995; Bankdonston, 1997; Centrie, 2000, 2004), El Salvadorians (C. Suarez-Orozco, 2000; M. Suarez-Orozco, 1997), as well as those from older immigrant communities such as Chinese (Sung, 1987; Suzuki, 1995) and South Asians (Leonard, 1997). Among the vast studies of immigrants, two distinct threads are discernible: (1) immigrant academic achievement and (2) the production of social identities. Both paralleling and departing from the above two major research foci is research related to the issue of keeping one's own language and the ways in which language maintenance and/or the lack thereof intersects with school performance and identity formation.

IMMIGRANT ACADEMIC ACHIEVEMENT

The majority of research addressing issues of immigrant students' performance in American schools focuses on K–12 public schools, especially secondary education. Research has shown encouraging evidence that, despite the social and economic disadvantages among the immigrant population as a whole, immigrant students often outperform their native peers in school. This phenomenon is known as the immigrant paradox. Meanwhile, research shows great academic variability among different immigrant groups (Crosnoe & Lopez Turley, 2011; Rumbaut & Portes, 2001; Suarez-Orozco, Bang, & Onaga, 2010), with immigrant paradox more pronounced among some Asian American groups and African immigrants

(Barringer, Takeuchi, & Xenos, 1090; Rumbaut & Ports, 2001; Kasinitz, Mollinkopf, Waters, & Holdaway, 2009). For some immigrant groups such as Mexicans, there is evidence of a negative correlation between academic achievement and years of residence in the United States; the longer they stay in the United States, the lower their academic achievement (Suarez-Orozco, 2000; M. Suarez-Orozco & C. Suarez-Orozco, 1995; Valenzuela, 1999).

John Ogbu's cultural-ecological theory has been the classical theory with respect to researchers' quest to explain differential academic achievement among varying minorities (Ogbu & Simons, 1998). This framework comprises two major parts: the "system," which refers to "the way minorities are treated or mistreated in education in terms of educational policies, pedagogy and returns for their investment on school credentials" (p. 3), and "community forces," which refers to "the way the minorities perceive and respond to schooling as a consequence of their treatment" (p. 3). The most influential part of this theory lies in its classification of minorities to explain the differences in school performance among minority groups. While the theory initially was an attempt to explain differences in Black/White/Mexican American achievement in school (Ogbu, 1982), Ogbu refined and broadened his framework over the years so that it now offers potential explanatory power for the achievement, or lack thereof, among varying immigrant groups. Numerous scholars interested in the subject of schooling and immigrants work with his framework, pushing it to be modified as it is tested on different groups and circumstances.

In the 1970s, educational researchers begin to examine the "mismatch" between the cultural background of ethnic minorities and the norms embedded within schools. Researchers explore how differences between home and school cultures affect the academic performance of minority youth, asserting that some minority students fail in school because school curricular and teacher practices are not responsive to nor educating them in relation to their culture or language (Trueba, 1998). Ogbu (1992) outlines this perspective as follows: (1) the content of the curriculum may be foreign to minority children, and therefore, it inhibits school learning from being reinforced in the home and community; (2) the method of teaching in school may be different from that within the home and/or community; (3) schooling may encourage children to aspire to goals that are out of their reach; and (4) schools may emphasize values that are in conflict with the values of the children's culture. Though public schools are often found to perpetuate racial inequality, culturally sensitive instruction and a trusting teacher-student relationship can make a difference in immigrant students' lives (Lee, 2005).

Researchers also look into contextual factors, including family background, community networks, language, and aspirations encouraged and developed in the home as affecting the academic achievement of immigrant children. Portes and MacLeod (1996), for example, find that both parental social economic status and ethnic community have significant independent effects on the second generation's academic performance. This result parallels that of other studies, including research on educational attainment among native-born American youth. In order to explain the effects of national background on academic achievement and attainment, they adopt Rumbaut and Portes's (2001) notion of "modes of incorporation," arguing that "these resilient effects can be interpreted as a reflection of the individual characteristics and different modes of incorporation experiences by first generation immigrants" (Portes & MacLeod, 1996, p. 270).

In addition to family background, social capital (human and information networks) is found to be important in relation to immigrant attainment. Stanton-Salazar and Dornbusch (1995) take a network analytic approach to analyzing the role of social capital in the underachievement of Mexican-origin high school students, emphasizing "the inequitable transmission of tangible institutional resources and opportunities" (p. 116) and the relationships with institutional agents. Aspirations are also found to be closely connected to social capital. In a classic study of Mexican and Cuban immigrants to the United States, results suggest that aspirations are set through a rational assessment of past attainments and skills, instead of the commonly assumed "dreams of fantasy" among new arrivals (Portes, MacLeod, & Parker, 1978). Hao and Bonstead-Bruns (1998) examine the relationship between social capital and parents and students' expectations. Given the relatively lower levels of parent–child interactions among the Chinese and Mexicans, they suggest that it is between-family social capital rather than within-family social capital that both directly and indirectly affects achievement among immigrant Chinese and Mexican students.

Also related to academic achievement among immigrant students is ethnic-language maintenance. Generally speaking, proficiency in one's ethnic language has a positive effect on school performance (Bankston & Zhou, 1995; Hao & Bonstead-Bruns, 1998; Valenzuela, 1999), suggestive of the fact that proximity to one's culture of origin predicts success in school (Centrie, 2004). However, the group that achieves highest academic accomplishment, the Chinese, is actually found to be the least likely to retain their parents' language (Kasinitz et al., 2009). Given the fact that Mandarin and Cantonese are gaining popularity in the United States, and that China is playing an increasingly important role in the global economy, the generational tension or family dynamic in terms of Chinese language retention would be an intriguing research topic.

Bankston and Zhou (1995) identify three major theoretical perspectives in native language literacy: forcible assimilation, reluctant bilingualism, and linguistic pluralism. Since the 1960s, the traditional assimilationist framework has been challenged, and a growing body of empirical evidence indicates the positive effect of bilingualism on cognitive abilities, scholastic achievement (Hao & Bonstead-Bruns, 1998; Portes & Schauffler, 1994), and ethnic self-identification. Bankston and Zhou (1995) find that minority students' literacy in their ethnic language is positively associated with academic achievement and identification with one's own ethnic group, contending that this is achieved through encouraging constructive forms of behavior because bilingualism gives students access to the social capital of a distinctive ethnic identity. Stanton-Salazar and Dornbusch (1995) denote a slight downside here, suggesting that although highly bilingual students may have an advantage over working-class English-dominant students in gaining access to adult social capital, even among those who are highly proficient in English, the use of Spanish continues to be associated with less than friendly relations with non-Mexican youth. Locke Davidson (1996) concludes similarly, based on her study of students of Mexican origin in California.

PRODUCTION OF SOCIAL IDENTITIES

Researchers investigating identity formation among varied immigrant groups take differing perspectives as their starting point. The first approach draws heavily upon Ogbu and looks at the production of social identity from a more macrolevel perspective (historical, economic, and/or political) and through the lens of group membership, asking how cultural differences or group minority status shape student and community behaviors and perceptions as related to schooling, ways of achieving success, and the groups' place in American society (Ogbu, 1987; Suarez-Orozco, 1997).

A second perspective looks into the daily practices of institutions, asking about the role schools and classrooms play in the making and molding of students' identities. Ann Locke Davidson's *Making and Molding Identity in Schools* (1996), for example, conceptualizes identity as "a process that develops in a matrix of structuring social and institutional relationships and practices" (p. 50), reframing the identity formation question so as to consider "the role of school and classroom practices in nurturing, resisting, or shaping the meanings students bring with them to school" (p. 3). In so doing, she encourages researchers to look into day-to-day school-based practices and processes in the analysis of student actions and processes of identity formation. Locke Davidson draws extensively upon work developed in the broader literature on the production of social identities, exploring carefully the ways in which Mexican American and Caucasian youth construct identities and the ways in which such identities are related to their academic performance and attainment. In addition, Angela Valenzuela

(1997) focuses carefully on both Mexican American youth who are new immigrants as well as those who are second or third generation, arguing strongly that the newcomers, in spite of language difficulties, often take school more seriously (1999, 2005).

Linking the above perspectives, a third perspective examines the dynamic between structural factors and institutional relationships and the influence of social factors in the assimilation of new immigrants within the school context. As Suarez-Orozco and Suarez-Orozco (1995) state: "The classroom is a microscopic version of the larger socioeconomic power structure, where teachers from the dominant majority culture and minority students communicate and interact in an environment of social inequality" (p. 59). Schools, they argue, "constitute institutional identities" among students, whereby any non-White ethnic identity is constituted as inferior. Carola Suarez-Orozco (2000) suggests that immigrant children are aware of the negative social images reflected in the school context and that, under such negative reflections, it is "extremely difficult to maintain an unblemished sense of self-worth for very long" (p. 213). Based on these findings, Suárez-Orozco (2001) develops the concept of "social mirroring" to illustrate how the host society's attitudes toward immigrant children, particularly those informed by discrimination and stereotypes, can affect immigrant children's identity formation.

Suarez-Orozco's (2001) findings are echoed in many studies. Ethnographic research on immigrant students in U.S. schools suggests that one of the first lessons such students learn about life in the U.S. concerns the existence of the racial hierarchy that places Whites at the top of the heap (Olsen, 1997). Through interaction with teachers and students, non-White immigrant students also learn that Whites are viewed as the only "real Americans" (Lee, 1996, 2005; Olsen, 1997). Stacey Lee's brilliant study on first- and second-generation Hmong American high school students sheds light on both "White culture" in school and the ways in which such culture influences immigrant minority students' identities. In her recent study (Lee, 2005), she finds that the culture of Whiteness/middle classness implicitly equates Whiteness with real Americans and is, therefore, viewed as better than all competing cultures/identities. Seen either as culturally different or culturally deficient, many Hmong American students are both academically and socially marginalized at the school while being simultaneously ideologically "blackened." Chinese Americans are, on the other hand, ideologically "whitened," reflective of and feeding into the "model minority myth."

The characterizations of Asian Americans as "model minorities" both parallels the notion of ideological whitening while simultaneously maintaining a Black–White racial binary (Park & Park, 1999), a binary that is challenged by both Asians and Latinos (Rodriguez, 1992, 1994). According to Ong (1999), the Black and White discourse on race frames the ways in which recent non-White immigrants are viewed by dominant society. Depending on their economic standing, immigrant groups are either ideologically White, such as middle class East Asians, or blackened, such as poor and working class immigrants and refugees. This interplay of forces demonstrates that race and class work together in the racialization of both Asian and Latino immigrants, a point which Lee (2005) picks up and extends in her later work.

In an effort to explain the varied paths of assimilation by different immigrant groups, Portes and Zhou (1993) theorize a "segmented assimilation." While some groups, such as European immigrants, follow a linear assimilation course and achieve high socioeconomic status, others experience backwardness and will be victim to long-term poverty. Gans (1992) also predicts a bleak future for second generation immigrants who are locked in poor inner-city schools and adopt urban youth culture. Some second-generation immigrants, in order to distance themselves from the social stigma that hovers over African Americans and Puerto Ricans most often, develop a distinctive identity. Waters (1999) argues, through her study of two generations of West Indian immigrants, that the economic edge that West Indians have over African Americans disappears by the second generation, wherein children are blocked by racism and discrimination. She suggests that only West Indian families who emphasize their identity as members of a distinct culture, thus resisting Americanization, avoid downward mobility, affirming the finding by numerous researchers that those children who remain closest to their culture of origin do best in school.

Alex Stepick (1998) argues strongly that it is the family's organization, sense of coherence, resources, and coping strategies (all of which he calls social capital) that predict differential academic and social outcomes among students who share the same social conditions, neighborhoods, and economic status. Zhou and Bankston (1998) conclude similarly, based on their studies of Vietnamese children, where they argue that community solidarity and cultural values related to family and school empower the Vietnamese second generation and allow these students to climb the social structure.

In general, research points to "selective acculturation" (Portes & Rumbaut, 2001) as the most successful immigrant practice, whereby immigrants have proficiency of English and the mainstream American norm while preserving aspects of their ethnic language and ties. Kasinitz et al.'s large-scale comparative project reports that, "Compared to past second generations, the children of immigrants today seem remarkably at ease about living between different worlds" (Kasinitz et al, 2009, p. 344).

CONCLUSION

Research on children of immigrants has been particularly vibrant over recent decades. Researchers on education of immigrants' children work within and across multiple fields and bring these various perspectives: psychological, sociological, anthropological, linguistic, and historical. Research in the field continues to benefit from theoretical frameworks ranging from more traditional status attainment models to critical theories to post-structuralism. Therefore, a body of work that sheds light on structural barriers for immigrants' status attainment as well as the varied lived experiences of subcategories of immigrant groups in terms of ethnicity, country of origin, and generation is emerging. This work contributes to our understanding of the experiences of immigrants' children and carries important policy implications.

From traditional assimilation theories to "segmented assimilation" (Portes & Zhou, 1993) and "selective acculturation" (Portes & Rumbaut, 2001), the past four decades have witnessed enormous theoretical development in immigrant research. Most recently, a special issue on immigration, youth, and education produced by *Harvard Education Review* proposed replacing the traditional terms—assimilation, adaptation, and acculturation—with the term transculturation (Oh & Cooc, 2001). Transculturation is a "developmental process that portrays children of immigrants as actors of merging and converging cultures in multidirectional and synchronous ways" (p. 401).

The last decade has produced some prominent research which utilized sophisticated methodological design, including longitudinal studies, in-depth ethnographic work, and large scale comparative projects. One such example is Carola and Marcelo Suarez-Orozco's book *Children of Immigration* (2001). This book centers on the five-year longitudinal Harvard Immigration Project, which follows 400 children from five different countries and regions: China, Mexico, Haiti, Central America, and the Dominican Republic. Some other recent influential work by Kasinitz and colleagues includes *Inheriting the City: The Children of Immigrants Come of Age* (Kasinitz et al., 2009) and its ethnographic counterpart *Becoming New Yorkers: Ethnographies of the New Second Generation* (Kasinitz, Mollenkopf, & Waters, 2006). The authors studied second-generation West Indians, Chinese, Dominicans, South Americans, and Russian Jews and compared them to Blacks, Whites, and Puerto Ricans with native-born parents. These works illuminate the field with their rich data, interdisciplinary perspectives, sophisticated methodological design, and theoretical significance.

So, where do we go from here? The author invites consideration of the following key points as we investigate into the education and lives of immigrants' children. We need to look more closely into the nexus of class, social capital, and gender issues in immigrant children's experiences. Some scholars have been looking at social capital in the forms of co-ethnic networks, local ethnic churches, and associations that help immigrants and their children succeed (Ablemann & Lie, 1995; Kwong, 1996). Also, scholars are pointing to the significance of class differences within ethnic enclaves (Li, 2010; Sanders & Nee, 1987). There is the need for more research that intersects ethnicity, class, and gender and examines these issues within the context of a new global economic and political terrain.

The restructuring of contemporary global capitalism brings about the global shift of economy and complicates the power relations among different actors—nations, schools, communities, ethnic groups, and so on. The world economic map has been redrawn (Dicken, 2007), and cultural, technological, and economic integration foster new opportunities and challenges for institutions and local lives. Transnationalism and global citizenship are emerging with new features (Portes, Guarnizo, & Landolt, 1999); multicultural education is in a new era; and the call for unity through diversity is loud and widespread in the United States. All these new global and domestic economic and political environments are closely affecting the immigrant children's experience and, therefore, should illuminate research. There is the need to look beyond the borders of schools and country to understand the new immigrants. A vital question must be asked: Under such a radically changing multidimensional context, how are individual and collective ethnic identities challenged, negotiated, and reconstructed? How are ethnicity, class, gender, and loci altered and realigned? What role are schooling and public policy playing in these construction and reconstruction processes? These difficult questions need to be answered as they address the important changes that are taking place. It is only at this price that it will be easier to situate studies on immigrants' children within these changing contexts. Understanding these issues is important not only to scholars of immigrant studies, but also to educators and policymakers, as all these processes are affecting and redefining the terrain where our immigrant children are navigating their futures. Immigrant children are a substantial and rapidly growing share of the American population, and their development, educational attainment, and integration into the country will play a defining role in the nation's future.

NOTES

1. The author uses "immigrants' children" to refer to immigrants' descendents—children and youth with at least one foreign born parent.
2. A version of this chapter was published as Sociology of Education in the United States, 1966–2008. In S. Tozer, B. Gallegos & A. Henry (Eds.), *Handbook of Research in the Social Foundations of Education*. New York: Routledge. The author thanks Dr. Lois Weis and Graduate School of Education at SUNY Buffalo for their support and advice on earlier versions of this chapter.
3. 2010 American Community Survey and Census Data, retrieved from http://www.migrationinformation.org/feature/display.cfm?ID=818#8

REFERENCES

Ableman, N., & Lie. J. (1995). *Blue dreams: Korean-Americans and the Los Angeles riots.* Cambridge, MA: Harvard University Press.

Bankston, C. L., III. (1997). Education and ethnicity in an urban Vietnamese village: The role of ethnic community involvement in academic achievement. In S. Maxine & L. Weis (Eds.), *Beyond black and white: New faces and voices in U.S. schools. SUNY Series, Power, Social Identity, and Education* (pp. 207–230). Albany, NY: State University of New York Press.

Bankston, C. L., & Zhou, M. (1995). Effects of minority-language literacy on the academic achievement of Vietnamese youths in New Orleans. *Sociology of Education, 68*(1), 1–17.

Barringer, H., Takeuchi, D., & Xenos, P. (1990). Education, occupational prestige, and income of Asian Americans. *Sociology of Education, 63*(1), 27–43.

Centrie, C. (2000). *Free spaces unfold: Families. community, and Vietnamese high school students' identities.* In L. Weis & M. Fine (Eds.), Construction sites: Excavating races, class, and gender among urban youth (pp. 65–83). New York, NY: Teachers College.

Centrie, C. (2004). *Identity formation of Vietnamese immigrant youth in an American high school.* New York, NY: LFB Scholarly.

Crosnoe, R., & Lopez Turley, R. N. (2011). K–12 educational outcomes of immigrant youth. *The Future of Children, 21*(2), 129–152. Retrieved from http://futureofchildren.org/futureofchildren/publications/journals/journal_details/index.xml?journalid=74

Dicken, P. (2007). *Global shift: Mapping the changing contours of the world economy.* Thousand Oaks, CA: Sage.

Fuller, B., Elmore, R. F., & Orfield, G. (Eds.). (1996). *Who chooses? Who cares? Culture institutions, and the unequal effects of school choice.* New York, NY: Teacher's College Press.

Gans, H. (1992). Second-generation decline: Scenarios for the economic and ethnic futures of the post-1965. *American Immigrants: Ethnic and Racial Studies, 15*(2), 173–192.

Hao, L., & Bonstead-Bruns, M. (1998). Parent–child differences in educational expectations and the academic achievement of immigrant and native students. *Sociology of Education, 71*(3), 175–198.

Kasinitz, P., Mollinkopf, J. H., & Waters, M. C. (2006). *Becoming New Yorkers: Ethnographies of the new second generation.* New York, NY: Russell Sage Foundation.

Kasinitz, P., Mollinkopf, J. H., Waters, M. C., & Holdaway, J. (2009). *Inheriting the city: The children of immigrants come of age.* New York, NY: Russell Sage Foundation.

Kwong, P. (1996). *The New Chinatown.* New York, NY: Hill and Wong.

Laguerre, M. S. (1997). Sex education among Haitian American adolescents. In M. Seller & L. Weis (Eds.), *Beyond black and white: New faces and voices in U.S. schools* (pp. 151–164). Albany, NY: State University of New York Press.

Lee, S. (1996). *Unraveling the "model minority" stereotype: Listening to Asian American youth.* New York, NY: Teachers College Press.

Lee, S. (2005). *Up against whiteness: Race, school, and immigrant youth*. New York, NY: Teachers College Press.

Leonard, K. (1997). Changing south Asian identities in the United States. In S. Maxine & L. Weis (Eds.), *Beyond black and white: New faces and voices in U.S. schools. SUNY Series, Power, Social Identity, and Education* (pp. 165–180). Albany, NY: State University of New York Press.

Li, G. (2010). Race, class, and schooling: Multicultural families doing the hard work of home literacy in America's inner city [Special Issue]. *Reading & Writing Quarterly, 28*(2), 140–165.

Locke Davidson, A. (1996). *Making and molding identity in schools: Student narratives on race, gender, and academic engagement*. Albany, NY: State University of New York Press.

Ogbu, J. (1987). Variability in minority school performance: A problem in search of an explanation. *Anthropology and Education Quarterly, 18*(4), 313–334.

Ogbu, J. (1992, June). *Understanding cultural differences and school learning*. Paper presented at the 83rd Annual Meeting of the Special Library Association, San Francisco, CA.

Ogbu, J., & Simons, H. (1998). Voluntary and involuntary minorities: A cultural-ecological theory of school performance with some implications for education. *Anthropology & Education Quarterly, 29*(2), 155–188.

Oh, S. S., & Cooc, N. (2011). Editor's introduction: Immigration, youth, and education. *Harvard Education Review, 81*(3), 397–406. Retrieved from http://her.hepg.org/content/w310738k22303n37/fulltext.pdf

Olsen, L. (1997). *Made in America: Immigrant students in our public schools*. New York, NY: New Press.

Ong, A. (1999). Cultural citizenship as subject making: Immigrants negotiate racial and cultural boundaries in the United States. In R. Torres, L. Miron, & J. Inda (Eds.), *Race, identity, and citizenship: A reader* (pp. 262–293). Malden, MA: Blackwell.

Orfield, G., & Lee, C. (2004). *Brown at 50: King's dream or Plessy's nightmare?* Cambridge, MA: Civil Rights Project, Harvard University. Retrieved from http://www.civilrightsproject.harvard.edu/research/reseg04/brown50.pdf

Park, E., & Park, J. (1999). A new American dilemma? Asian Americans and Latinos in race theorizing. *Journal of Asian American Studies, 2*(3), 289–309.

Pessar, P. R. (2001) Dominicans: Transnational identities and local politics. In Nancy Foner (Ed.), *New immigrants in New York* (pp. 251–274). New York, NY: Columbia University Press.

Portes, A., Guarnizo, L., & Landolt, P. (1999). The study of transnationalism: Pitfalls and promise of an emergent research field. *Ethnic and Racial Studies, 22*(2), 217-237.

Portes, A., & MacLeod, D. (1996). Educational progress of children of immigrants: The roles of class, ethnicity, and school context. *Sociology of Education, 69*(4), 255–275.

Portes, A., MacLeod, S. A., & Parker, R. N. (1978). Immigrant aspirations. *Sociology of Education, 51*(4), 241–260.

Portes, A., & Rumbaut, L. (2001). *The story of the immigrant second generation*. Berkeley, CA: University of California Press.

Portes, A., & Schauffler, R. (1994). Language and the second generation. In R. G. Rumbaut & S. Pedrazgo (Eds.), *International Migration Review, 28*, 640–641. New York, NY: Wadsworth.

Portes, A., & Zhou, M. (1993). Should immigrants assimilate? *Public Interest, 116*, 18–33.

Rodriguez, C. (1992). Race, culture and Latino "otherness" in the 1980 Census. *Social Science Quarterly, 73*(4), 930–937.

Rodriguez, C. (1994). Challenging racial hegemony: Puerto Ricans in the United States. In S. Gregory & R. Sanjek (Eds.), *Race* (pp. 131–145). New Brunswick, NJ: Rutgers University Press.

Rong, X., & Brown, F. (2001). The effects of immigrant generation and ethnicity on educational attainment among young African and Caribbean Blacks in the United States. *Harvard Educational Review, 71*(3), 475–504.

Rong, X., & Brown, F. (2002). Socialization, culture and identities of Black immigrant children. *Education and Urban Society, 34*(2), 247–347.

Rumbaut, R. G., & Portes, A. (Eds.). (2001). *Ethnicities: Children of immigrants in America*. Berkeley, CA: University of California Press.

Rumberger, R. (1983). Dropping out of high school: The influence of race, sex, and family background. *American Educational Research Journal, 20*(2), 199–220.

Rumberger, R. (1995). Dropping out of middle school: A multilevel analysis of students and schools. *American Educational Research Journal, 32*(3), 583–625.

Rumberger, R., & Thomas, S. (2000). The distribution of dropout and turnover rates among urban and suburban high schools. *Sociology of Education, 73*(1), 39–67.

Sanders, J. M., & Nee, V. (1987). Limits of ethnic solidarity in the enclave economy. *American Sociological Review, 52*, 745–767.

Seller, M., & Weis, L. (Eds.). (1997). *Beyond black and white: New faces and voices in U.S. schools*. Albany, NY: State University of New York Press.

Stanton-Salazar, R. D., & Dornbusch, S. M. (1995). Social capital and the reproduction of inequality: Information networks among Mexican-origin high school students. *Sociology of Education, 68*(2), 116–135.

Stepick, A. (1998). *Pride against prejudice: Haitians in the United States*. Boston, MA: Allyn and Bacon.

Suarez-Orozco. C., Bang. H.. & Onaga. M. (2010, November). Contributions to variations in academic trajectories amongst recent immigrant youth. *International Journal of Behavioral Development*.

Suarez-Orozco, C. (2000). Identities under siege: Immigration stress and social mirroring among the children of immigrants. In C. G. M. Robben & M. Suarez-Orozco (Eds.), *Cultures under siege: Collective violence and trauma* (pp. 194–226). New York, NY: Cambridge University Press.

Suarez-Orozco, C., & Suarez-Orozco, M. (2002). *Children of immigration*. Cambridge, MA: Harvard University Press.

Suarez-Orozco, M. M. (1997). Becoming somebody: Central American immigrants in U.S. inner city schools. In S. Maxine & L. Weis (Eds.), *Beyond black and white. New faces and voices in U.S. schools. SUNY Series, Power, Social Identity, and Education* (pp. 115–130). Albany, NY: State University of New York Press.

Suarez-Orozco, M., & Suarez-Orozco, C. (1995). *Transformations: Immigration, family life, and achievement motivation among Latino adolescents*. Stanford, CA: Stanford University Press.

Sung, B. L. (1987). *The adjustment experience of Chinese immigrant children in New York City*. Staten Island, NY: Center Migration Studies.

Suzuki, B. H. (1995). Education and the socialization of Asian Americans: A revisionist analysis of the "model minority" thesis. In D. T. Nakanishi & T. Y. Nishida (Eds.), *The Asian American educational experience: A source book for teachers and students* (pp. 113–132). New York, NY: Routledge.

Trueba, H. (1998). *Raising silent voices: Educating the linguistic minorities for the 21st century*. Cambridge, MA: Newbury House.

Valenzuela, A. (1999). *Subtractive schooling: U.S.—Mexican youth and the politics of caring*. Albany, NY: State University of New York Press.

Waters, M. (1999). *Black identities: West Indian immigrant dreams and American realities*. New York, NY: Russell Sage Foundation/Cambridge, MA: Harvard University Press.

Zhou, M., & Bankston, C. L., III. (1998). *Growing up American: How Vietnamese children adapt to life in the United States*. New York, NY: Russell Sage Foundation.

CHAPTER 3

MAINSTREAMING NEW IMMIGRANT STUDENTS

The Struggles of an African 5th Grader

Esther Somé-Guiébré

The issues regarding language and minority students in the classroom have often been linked to the marginalization of their linguistic and cultural background in their school setting (Gonzales, 2005; Ogbu & Simmons, 1998), their age at immigration, the language of their countries of origin, their communities of residence, their pre- and postimmigration experiences (Espenshade & Fu, 1997), and classroom practices (Harklau, 1994; Nieto, 2002; Valdes, 2001). The existing literature, however, discusses issues regarding children from Hispanic and Asian backgrounds, while issues regarding African immigrant children remain unexplored. Besides, African immigrant students are often invisible in school data. They are lumped into the larger group of African Americans, English language learners, or simply immigrant students. This minimizes the presence of that student population and could account for their slow academic, social, cultural, and linguistic adaptation in the classroom.

In this chapter, I examine the nature of the relationship between Sally (an African immigrant student), her peers, and her mainstream classroom

Immigration and Schooling: Redefining the 21st Century America, pp. 39–54

teacher, and how those were connected to classroom instructional practices. I use the term mainstream teacher to refer to homeroom teachers. As Sally's mainstream teacher, Mrs. Parks taught all students in the same classroom, including English language learners (ELLs), American-born citizens, and students with disabilities.

Sally and her family moved from the Democratic Republic of Congo, a former Belgian colony, to the United States as permanent residents only five months prior to my data collection. Immigration and permanent residency were granted to her family through the Diversity Visa Lottery organized yearly by the United States government. Prior to immigration, she spoke Lingala and French, but had no exposure to the English language. Soon after immigration, Sally was placed into Mrs. Parks' 5th-grade classroom that already included two African immigrant students—Carine, also from the Democratic Republic of Congo, and Bintou from Liberia. All three girls attended an English as a second language (ESL) class. Bintou and Sally attended the same ESL class and were pulled out twice a day for a higher-level English language literacy class, while Carine was only pulled out once.

Not unlike most of the African immigrant students' families in her school, Sally's parents were educated Africans who left their home country for the United States in the hope of better living conditions and educational opportunities. African immigrants are often disillusioned after immigration, as the linguistic, social, and cultural background of their children is often marginalized and delegitimized at school (Somé-Guiebré, 2011). Like her African peers, Sally was struggling to adapt herself to the new social and cultural setting of her school. I purposely chose Sally for this paper as she was the newest African student participant I had. I believe that her experience will enlighten the reader on the issues faced by African immigrants in the classroom on a daily basis.

THEORETICAL FRAMEWORK

Sally spoke at least two languages, Lingala, her native language, and French, the official language of her home country. She brought into the classroom a cultural capital that was "in-between spaces" (Bhabha, 1994) because of the influence of the colonial experience in her country. Bhabha (1994) argues that in the in-between space, "space and time cross to produce complex figures of difference and identity, past and present, inside and outside, inclusion and exclusion" (p. 2). Immigration complicates African children's sense of belonging, as they are not in a position to identify themselves solely in relation to their cultural and linguistic background. They are, instead, part of a hybrid cultural space in which "the borderline work of culture demands an encounter with newness that is not part of past and present" (Bhabha, 1994, p. 10). The cultural differences brought by Sally ought to be considered in her classroom as boundaries, and that would imply that Sally's teacher builds on her experiences to enhance her learning (Erickson, 2007). Teachers, however, are being prepared for monolingual students, and they can hardly meet the needs of the growing number of English language learners (ELLs) in classrooms (Nieto, 2002), no matter how good their intentions are. The disregard for their linguistic and cultural diversity isolates them and results in poor academic achievement. The same argument holds for both ESL and mainstream teachers, who, according to Harklau (1994), lead classroom discussions while students' participation is limited to a single word or phrase. Limited classroom interaction reduces students' opportunity to practice communicative strategies, and their productivity is less likely to be elicited.

Building on Sally's cultural experiences presupposes the existence of a social and educational relationship between her and her teacher. However, according to her teacher, Sally is not a very social student. I argue that Sally's lack of apparent social skills is rooted in classroom discriminatory practices, not necessarily intentional. Discrimination is a "negative or destructive behavior that can result in denying some groups' life's necessities as well as privileges, rights, and opportunities enjoyed by other groups" (Nieto, 2000, p. 34). It is the exclusion and the deprivation of people from the rights and opportunities available to all. It is based on privileging the attitudes and beliefs of some people over a group of people.

METHODOLOGY

This was a naturalistic study using descriptive data and participants' perspectives (Bogdan & Biklen, 2007). Observing classroom interactions as they occur on a regular basis was useful to the understanding of the interactions between the different parties in the classroom as well as the challenges and opportunities offered to each one of them. The study allowed me to understand the actions observed in the historical context of the setting.

Study Site and Participants

The data were collected in a Midwestern elementary school with a student population that was mostly White (41.3%), followed by Blacks (33.5%), Asian (16.5%), Hispanic (8.3%), and Native American (0.5%). The Black population included 10 students who were mostly natives of French-speaking African countries. This study is part of a larger project that involved three classrooms. In this chapter, I only refer to data collected in a 5th-grade classroom of 19 students including Sally, Bintou, and Carine, who all hailed from Africa. Sally and Carine were from the Congo, where they received formal education in French and spoke both French and Lingala, as mentioned earlier. As for Bintou, she was from Liberia and she only spoke English. Although the three girls were pulled out of their mainstream classroom for ESL, Carine was only pulled out once at the end of the day for 40 minutes, while the other two girls were pulled out twice for 40 minutes each time because of their low level of literacy in the English language.

As for Mrs. Parks, the 5th-grade teacher, she had been teaching for three years at the time of data collection. Throughout the three years, she taught students of diverse backgrounds. However, Carine, Bintou, and Sally were her first exposure to African students. Finally, Mrs. Rogers, Bintou and Sally's ESL teacher, had been practicing for five years, and this was also her first exposure to African students.

Data Sources

As data collection methods in this study, I used observation field notes, audiotapes, and interviews. I observed Sally's classroom three days a week for a month from 8.30 a.m. to 2.00 p.m. I observed her both in her mainstream and ESL classrooms. Observing classroom discussions allowed me to immerse in the lives of my participants in order to have a deeper grasp of their experiences and their perspectives (Emerson, Fretz, & Shaw, 1995). I audiotaped the discussions and transcribed them. This was instrumental in understanding the interactions between the two parties. The last method of data collection was semi-structured interviews involving two teachers (Mrs. Parks and Mrs. Rogers). I also had informal conversations with Sally, Carine, and Bintou. The interviews deepened my understanding of the events and activities observed and helped me make sense of the findings from the perspective of the participants.

The Researcher's Role

As a researcher, I was somewhat of an insider because, as an African woman and mother of two children, I got to experience some of the issues and frustrations caused by the cultural and social displacement of immigrant families in schools. On the other hand, I was an outsider to my research because of my status in the U.S. as a "stranger" (Simmel, 2008). As a stranger, I was certainly not familiar (at least practically) either with classroom practices in the United States, or with American cultural norms and values.

In a discussion about the role of the ethnographer in her study, Villenas (2010) shared her complex position in her study as the colonizer and the colonized. As a person of color, she was "the colonized in relation to the greater society, to the institution of higher learning, and to the dominant majority culture in the research setting" (p. 347). She identified herself as "a colonized" because she was a Chicana navigating a society dominated by White mainstream cultures. Not unlike Villenas, I was myself "a colonized" struggling to find my own way through the mainstream American culture in order to understand and grasp my hybrid identity (Bhabha, 1994) and that of my student participants. My hybrid identity created through my historical colonial background and my postimmigration experiences doubled with my race and my continent of origin could explain the strong bonds between the students and me. That connection eased the way for great rapport between the student participants and me. I was also "the colonizer because I am the educated, 'marginalized' researcher, recruited and sanctioned by privileged dominant institutions to write for and about Latino communities" (Villenas, 2010, p. 347). As someone accredited by a dominant institution to investigate African students, I also represented the image of the oppressor and was often perceived as another teacher by the African students.

Decision Making

The choice of the site was determined through a purposive sampling. It was assigned to me by the Bureau of Educational Office and was based on the presence of my target population in the school. Once I accessed the school, I first discussed with the principal who suggested four potential classrooms. However, two of the classrooms only had one African student each. I had decided to spend more time in the two classrooms that had two or more African students.

Data Analysis

The data analysis procedure used to discuss the findings is inductive (Dyson & Genishi, 2005) in nature. I grounded the analysis in the data gathered during the observation sessions, the interviews, and the textual analysis. I started the analysis with a reading of my field notes and interview transcripts and making comments about them. A second round of reading allowed me to identify recurrent themes and topics and led to the organization of those themes into categories for coding purposes (Patton, 1990). I used thematic units of analysis that consisted of a cross-case analysis of the interviews "by grouping together answers from different people to common questions or analyzing different perspectives on central issues" (Patton, 1990, p. 376). It also involved the organization of the observation data around key issues and or themes.

Interactions Between Sally and her Peers and Teachers

In a discussion about affirming diversity, Nieto (2000) argued that English language learners are physically and emotionally separated from their peers who are native English speakers. Although Sally spent a lot of time in her mainstream classroom, she was mostly emotionally and linguistically separated from her peers. Her relationship with them was most of the time limited to her interaction with Carine and Bintou, the two other African students in her classroom. In the following conversation I had with her, I enquired about the nature of her relationship with her peers.

Interviewer:	Why are you not playing with the other students?
Sally:	I told you, they don't like to play with me.
Interviewer:	Why do you say that?
Sally:	They insult me.
Interviewer:	What do they say?
Sally:	I don't know. Even those girls wearing yellow and blue (she pointed at two girls chatting), they are mean. When I look at them, they do like that.... (She blinked)
Interviewer:	What does that mean?
Sally:	I don't know.
Interviewer:	How about Carine? Can you play with her?
Sally:	She only talks to me on the bus in the morning. When we are at school, she does not want to talk to me. (I address the reason why Carine does not talk to Sally later in the paper)
Interviewer:	How about Bintou?
Sally:	She is not smart.
Interviewer:	Really?
Sally:	She always asks me to help her write things in ESL. But, when we come to class, she becomes mean.

This vignette clearly unveils the disconnect between Sally and her peers, a disconnect apparently caused by Sally's limited English proficiency. Her linguistic limitations created a social and cultural barrier that convinced her that her peers did not like her and even led them to make fun of her. Her teacher, Mrs. Parks, attributed the disconnect to the fact that she "is more socially immature than the other kids.... She comes to school where most of the students are more sexually aware, physically more mature than she is. And so she kind of ... likes Barbies and she is still more naïve than the other kids." Mrs. Rogers, her ESL teacher, made a similar comment and said that she was socially "a little bit behind 5th grade.... I attribute it to 5th grade. I think they [Sally's peers] are going through puberty, they are going to middle school. They are in a very different place right now. She [Sally] seems more like a 2nd or 3rd grader."

Although I am not discarding Mrs. Parks and Mrs. Rogers' perception of the disconnect between Sally and her peers, I point the finger to factors related to her knowledge of the English language and to how she is treated in the classroom. I argue that not having the flexibility of the English language was a major impediment to her interaction with her peers. She only interacted with them during activities that did not request an extensive use of the English language. The only time I observed her interact with her peers (three weeks after I started my data collection), was the day when the class had gone on a trip to a neighborhood playground for "Fun Friday" (a twenty-minute activity during which the class went to the neighborhood park). The students, including Sally, were running up and down the slides laughing and trying to catch each other. The few sentences I heard were, "I'll catch you," "No, you won't," "Wait!" "What are you doing?" I told Mrs. Park that it was the first time that I caught Sally interacting with other students and she responded that, whenever they were at the playground, there was not a lot of conversation going on and Sally was often playing with them. Her limited fluency in English reduced her ability to interact with her peers and convinced her that her peers did not like her or that they made fun of her.

Her inability to communicate with them rendered her sense of identification to her school and classroom environment difficult and reinforced her connection with her home environment. Sally's sense of identification is consistent with Portes and McLeod (1996), who maintain that the more fluent in English immigrant students are, the more they identify with the American culture. In fact, in a study about Francophone African immigrants in Canada, Ibrahim (1999) highlights the fact that those students face peer pressure and are denigrated when they do not speak English fluently. He also adds that they view English as "a source of pride" (p. 359) and turn to popular culture to acquire the English language to shape their lives and identities.

Unlike the participants in Ibrahim's study, Sally looked for comfort in her home setting. Home was the one place that provided the security and comfort she needed. In the home setting, Sally found people who looked like her, spoke the same languages, and understood her. There was no social, linguistic, or even cultural wall between her and her home environment. It was a safe environment that accepted her and did not pressure her to adapt or assimilate. Sally expressed her comfort in her home setting through her writing assignment. While her peers often discussed their friendships and interests in shopping, TV shows, and football in their writings, Sally always wrote about her parents and her siblings. Her confinement to her home betrays the fact that she had yet to develop a hybrid sense of identity. Although she was well on her way of being "in between spaces" (Bhabha, 1994), her fluency in the English language hindered her interaction with her peers, therefore slowing down her learning processes. In fact, Ibrahim (1999) argues that "popular culture, especially friendship, and peer pressure, all hasten the speed of learning" (p. 359).

The issue with Sally's interactions was also prompted by the nature of classroom instruction. In fact, classroom instructions were often designed to exclude those students who were judged unable to comprehend content. During a writing assignment, Mrs. Parks requested that the students write stories of their choice in their journals. When the students finished writing their stories, she read them, underlined the misspelled words, inquired about the meaning of some words and engaged them in a one-on-one conversation about their papers. When it was Sally's turn, however, she read it quietly, did not do any correction and did not ask her any question. Instead, she gave it back to her and complimented her on a job well done. Although the writing assignment was an opportunity for Mrs. Parks to converse and interact with her students, the conversation did not happen with Sally. On the one hand, Mrs. Parks did encourage Sally through her statement "very nice," but on the other, she implied a lack of interest in her writing and failed to establish a communicative relationship with her student. Her approach to Sally's writing reinforced Sally's low self-confidence, convincing her of her inferiority vis-à-vis the rest of the class. Mrs. Parks has hence contributed to disempowering Sally through her perceptions, beliefs, and thinking (Colville-Hall, McDonald, & Smolen, 1995).

During a language arts class, Mrs. Parks asked Sally to go to a computer and use her headphones to listen to books. For the next 50 minutes, Sally listened to books on the computer while her peers had language arts and then mathematics. The reading activity was unguided, isolated, and purposeless. It involved neither any contextual information nor any vocabulary or guided discussion. The lack of guided activity betrayed Mrs. Parks' only motive, which was to occupy Sally and separate her from the rest of the class. She denied Sally the opportunity to interact with the readings and hindered the communicative focus of reading comprehension. A communicative approach would allow Sally to answer and ask questions about the texts and then support her journey towards literacy development (Iddings, Risko, & Rampulla, 2009). Through the two activities discussed above, Mrs. Parks clearly uncovered her belief that Sally was incapable of acquiring content knowledge because of her limited fluency in the English language. In doing so, she not only limited Sally's learning opportunities, but she also created a barrier between Sally and the rest of the class.

In a discussion about funds of knowledge, Erickson (2007) urged teachers to view cultural diversity as boundaries and not as borders. The view of Sally's cultural and linguistic difference as a boundary would have facilitated her integration in the classroom and initiated a successful learning experience for her. It does, however, appear that Sally's difference was viewed as a border, which marginalized her from the rest of the class and reinforced the existing structures of inequalities in schools.

Sally's marginalization spotlights the fact that her teacher did not view her linguistic and cultural background as a resource (Verplaetse & Migliacci, 2008) and did not find it necessary to develop instructional strategies that would be inclusive of her needs. In a discussion about culturally relevant pedagogies, Ladson-Billings (2007) stressed the need for teachers to believe in the abilities of their students to perform, consider themselves as members of a community, view their teaching practice as an art, and resist the isolation of students according to their social, economic, and cultural background. It is arguably the case that Mrs. Parks had little or no belief in Sally's abilities and did not expect her to be a successful learner and, therefore, granted her the permission to fail (Ladson-Billings, 2002).

Another argument is that Mrs. Park's low expectation for Sally disempowered her and convinced her of her limited potential in achieving in class. In their discussion of "Pygmalion in the Classroom," Rosenthal and Jacobson (1968) note that "it is possible that teachers react to children of all grade levels in the same way if they believed them to be capable of intellectual gain" (p. 20). In light of the nature of the relationship between Sally and her teacher, it is fair to say that Mrs. Parks' low expectation communicated very low expectations about Sally's ability to learn effectively. In fact, if in her ESL classroom, Sally was very vocal and active, in her main classroom, she was a passive learner who rarely showed interest in what the rest of the class was doing. Sally's active participation in her ESL classroom was in part motivated by the small number of students (only three), which made it easier for the teacher to focus on each student's individual needs. In fact, Belete, Hamza, and Somé (2008) argue that African immigrant students are indebted to their ESL teachers "who go out of their way to equip them with this basic tool (English) to function in the American society" (p. 33).

Yet, the major issue with Sally's enrollment in ESL was that her ESL instructions mostly excluded content knowledge and focused exclusively on basic literacy development. Conversely, literacy development is more significant when accompanied with comprehensible input. According to Barrera (1983), reading is acquired in context through comprehension and is not conditioned by the level of fluency. In Barrera's view, literacy development ought to be inclusive of content knowledge, which, according to Garcia (2003), would allow the student to develop "the necessary vocabulary and linguistic structures relevant to the domain" (p. 43). Unfortunately, although ESL allowed Sally to develop some basic communicative literacy skills, the lack of content knowledge denied her the opportunity to acquire the English language while learning the course contents of her grade level.

Sally's exposure to content knowledge was made difficult as she was consistently pulled out of her mainstream classroom in the middle of one subject, only to come back in the middle of another subject twice a day. Hence, she was never in her mainstream classroom long enough to be exposed to the 5th grade curriculum in math, science, social studies, and so on, and she did not have any of them in ESL. Her inadequate involvement with academic learning placed her at a disadvantage with her peers, who had the opportunity to follow the full instructions. It reinforced the implicit and misguided assumption that Sally was not capable of understanding content knowledge without a significant amount of English language fluency. Her linguistic abilities were considered as deficits, and she was denied the possibility to develop her English language literacy in the context of content learning. Neither one of her teachers took responsibility for her learning. Although they did not make negative comments about her, they considered her immigration status to be at fault (Sleeter, 2005), a problem in need of a solution.

SALLY'S RESPONSE TO MARGINALIZATION

I argue that the relationship between Sally and Mrs. Parks reflected Bourdieu's notion of symbolic violence, which is an unconscious exertion of domination over conscious beings. It can only be "exerted on a person predisposed (in his habitus) to feel it, whereas others will ignore it" (Bourdieu, 1991, p. 51). Sally responded to the symbolic violence imposed on her through her passivity and physical and emotional detachment from the rest of the class. Following Cummins' (2000) discussion of coercive relation of power, Sally's passivity and physical separation were a form of resistance to the power relationships imposed on her. Coercive relation of power, according to Cummins, implies that a dominant group imposes its power to the detriment of the subordinate group who submits to the dominant one and adopts its values and norms. Sally was not passive to the coercion exercised on her in her classroom. She took matters in her own hands to deal with the coercion and became an agent of her own marginalization, thus reducing her learning opportunities.

Sally also responded to the coercion imposed on her through an attempt to distinguish herself from Bintou, another African student in her class. Although Bintou had been living in the United States for two years, she attended the same ESL class level as Sally. She was lagging behind her peers, and even behind Sally, who was a newcomer in the United States. She was more fluent in English than Sally and was expected to participate in classroom activities, although she never really did. The relationship between the two girls was mostly apparent in ESL, where the teacher often requested them to work together. Sally found out in her ESL classrooms that, although she was not fluent in English, she was doing better than Bintou. That knowledge boosted her self-confidence, but also led her to engage in a constant struggle to prove that she was better. The issue between Sally and Bintou is about language and power. The English language fluency empowered Bintou, who was able to take advantage of the American social, linguistic, and cultural environment (Collins & Blot, 2003). On the other hand, it disempowered Sally, who was denied learning privileges, rights, and opportunities (Nieto, 2000).

Sally's reaction towards Bintou was triggered by her teacher's discrimination against her on the basis of her inadequate language fluency. The discrimination uncovers the fact that Mrs. Parks was yet to develop culturally responsive pedagogies that would allow her to take advantage of her immigrant students' cultural and linguistic background in her teaching.

The discrimination against Sally is consistent with Nieto's (2000) definition. Discrimination for her is a "negative or destructive behavior that can result in denying some groups' life's necessities as well as privileges, rights, and opportunities enjoyed by other groups" (p. 34). It is the exclusion of Sally and the deprivation from the rights and opportunities available to all. Following Nieto's definition, the discrimination against Sally is based on Mrs. Parks' attitudes and beliefs about Sally. It has prompted the difficult nature of the relationship between Sally and her peers and her thirst to prove herself better than Bintou, who was expected to participate in class.

Another issue raised from the conversation above was related to the relationship between Sally and Carine, the other African student in her class, who was fluent in English and spoke the same languages Sally spoke (Lingala and French). According to Sally, Carine only talked to her on the bus and not at school. Sally's observation sounded exaggerated to me at first, as I had seen the two girls talk before. However, as I reviewed my notes, I realized that the interaction between the two girls was often based on a translation or explanation of facts. For instance, when the teachers and/or school administrators wanted to talk to Sally or send a message to her parents, they requested Carine for translation. It was also common to see Sally ask questions about activities done in class. For instance, Sally once showed a handout about caves to Carine during class, asking her what it was in Lingala. Carine responded to her, and Sally asked another question, to which Carine said, "I don't know." According to Mrs. Parks, Carine did not always want to be the translator, and that made Sally feel left out. She also added that Carine was often immature, forgot that Sally did not speak English, and always wanted to interact with the other girls. Ms. Li, the teacher in charge of Mrs. Parks' class at recess in the school argued,

> It's been a difficult situation for Sally because we [the school] anticipated that because she [Carine] had to be the "teacher," her teacher putting her in the role of what an adult interpreter would do, she is frustrated with that. She was very willing to help. I've had students who I asked to help; they said no they don't wanna do it. They wanna speak English only.... But I think that it becomes some sort of a burden.... Carine is frustrated having to translate everything to Sally and Sally is frustrated because she doesn't understand. These are things we knew were going to happen but you know it's better to have something, especially for Sally.

As Ms. Li argued above, Sally's dependence on Carine for interactions with her teachers and peers was a burden to the latter and frustrated the two of them. Although Carine was often willing to do the translation, it did create a gap between the two girls; one of them was perceived as needy, or inferior, and the other one as privileged. Sally's dependence on Carine's translation services raises the issue of power relationships once again. As an immigrant student who is fluent and integrated into her classroom, Carine was already "in between" spaces. Being in between spaces provided her with the "terrain of elaborating strategies of selfhood—singular or communal—that initiate a new sign of identity and innovative sites of collaboration and contestation in the act of society itself" (Bhabha, 1994, p. 2). Being in between spaces facilitated the authoritative role provided to her in her classroom. She represented the teacher, the "norm," while Sally is still and always the "other." As the teacher, she reproduced the structure put in place in her classroom.

IMPLICATIONS FOR TEACHER EDUCATION

This study has several implications, mostly for teachers and teacher educators. Teachers need to be mindful of the power relationships in classrooms and their implications for all students in general, and immigrant students in particular. An understanding of the power relations in the classroom would allow teachers to develop instructional strategies that would create a space for social adaptation and academic achievement. It would, for instance, create a collaborative relation of power and, therefore, reduce or minimize any form of resistance.

Furthermore, teacher education programs should emphasize the necessity for teachers to understand the challenges faced by their immigrant students, not through their own privileged standpoint, but through the standpoint of the students and their socioeconomic realities. Sleeter (2005) states, "Teachers who take responsibility for student learning recognize challenges students and their families face, but are convinced that those challenges do not prevent learning and that a strong education will serve students" (p. 128). Doing so would minimize stereotypes and discrimination that can magnify students' low self-confidence, causing them to lag far behind their peers.

Besides, teacher education programs should help student teachers develop an understanding of immigrant students' sense of identity. Although teachers may be aware of cultural and racial differences, they might not have a full understanding of how hybridity comes into play in immigrant students' learning practices. An understanding of immigrant student's sense of identity entails a view of students' first language as a resource for learning instead of a handicap (Sleeter, 2005).

Another implication of this study is related to the connection between ESL and mainstream classrooms. As the findings suggest, Sally had an inconsistent exposure to content knowledge. That inconsistency was in part due to ESL pullout that took place in the middle of content knowledge and the almost exclusive focus of ESL instruction on superficial literacy. It is thus essential that mainstream and ESL teachers establish a collaborative relationship between the two instructional spaces and, hence, create a more positive learning environment for immigrant students. It is also essential that ESL teachers include subject matter knowledge in their literacy instructions. As a matter of fact, Garcia (2003) argues that content knowledge exposure allows English language learners to develop "the necessary vocabulary and linguistic structures relevant to the domain" (p. 43).

According to Lucas, Villegas, and Freedson-Gonzalez (2008), "to be successful with ELLs, ... teachers need to draw on established principles of second language learning" (p. 362). Mainstream teachers need to be equipped with knowledge of second language literacy development. Such awareness would provide them with the necessary tools to address the linguistic challenges of their immigrant student populations. For instance, it would allow them to view students' first language of literacy as an asset and use it for an effective development of literacy in English. In the same vein, knowledge in second language literacy would allow teachers to develop strategies to include ELLs in instruction, even when the latter have not yet developed the English fluency skills deemed necessary for instruction.

What about a district-wide policy in schools consisting of providing translators for ESL students? It is not convenient to use students as translators. Even if they were willing to do so, it is damaging to the self-esteem of the students in need and, at the same time, it steals their instruction time away.

CONCLUSION

In this chapter, I investigated the relationship between Sally, her peers, and her mainstream teacher, as well as some of the factors that facilitated or impeded her interaction with her peers. I claim that Sally was marginalized from the rest of her class. Her marginalization was triggered, among other things, by her lack of fluency in English. Unlike her American peers and the other two African students in her classroom, Sally was still struggling to learn English, and that seriously limited her ability to converse with her peers and with her teacher. Classroom instructional practices were also the culprits in Sally's marginalization. Mrs. Parks discriminated against Sally on the basis of her language fluency, denied her of content knowledge, and excluded her de facto from classroom interactions.

From a postcolonial perspective, the power relationship between Sally and her teacher prompted the discrimination against her. She was submitted to an uneven relationship of power. Her teacher was unwittingly influenced by a deficit model with regard to Sally's cultural and linguistic "handicaps." This perception of Sally's background hindered her ability to smoothly transition to the in-between space that could have empowered her in her struggles for adaptation (Collins & Blot, 2003). From a critical perspective, the classroom practices deployed in Sally's classroom failed to challenge the hegemonic relations of power encouraged through multicultural education. Instead, those practices reinforced educational inequalities, prejudices, stereotypes, and discrimination. The uneven power relationships, discrimination, and marginalization of Sally prompted her isolation from social interactions, which translated into a slower process of meaningful literacy development.

The issues discussed in this chapter reveal a lack of clear framework within which to deal with English language learners, and African students in particular. Given that most mainstream teachers are not equipped with theoretical and practical knowledge necessary to serve the needs of ELLs, schools should encourage their teachers to take courses or participate in workshops that will endow them with culturally and linguistically responsive instructional strategies. Such courses might compel them to examine and address power relationships in classrooms in ways that can minimize the marginalization and discrimination against immigrant students. Schools also need to be aware that relying on one student to serve as a translator for another can be very disadvantageous for both students as it burdens the translator and perpetuates the dependency of the less fluent student. Schools should explore other avenues for providing students with translation services.

REFERENCES

Barrera, R. (1983). Bilingual reading in the primary grades: Some questions about questionable views and practices. In T. H. Escobedo (Ed.), *Early childhood bilingual education: A Hispanic perspective* (pp. 164–183). New York, NY: Teachers College Press.

Belete, M. B, Hamza, H., & Somé, T. H. (2008). Educating the African new comer student in Western New York: The case of SIFE and multilingual learners. In C. S. Sunal & K. Mutua (Eds.), *Undertaking educational challenges in the 21st century: Research from the field* (pp. 23–46). Charlotte, NC: Information Age.

Bhabha, H. (1994). *The location of culture*. New York, NY: Routlege.

Bogdan, R. C., & Biklen, S. K. (2007). *Qualitative research for education: An introduction to theory and methods*. Boston, MA: Allyn & Bacon.

Bourdieu, P. (1991). *Language and symbolic power*. Boston, MA: Harvard University Press.

Colville-Hall, S., MacDonald, S., & Smolen, L. (1995). Preparing preservice teachers for diversity in learners. *Journal of Teacher Education, 46*, 295–303.

Collins, J., & Blot, R. (2003). *Literacy and literacies: Texts, power, and identity*. Cambridge, UK: Cambridge University Press.

Cummins, J. (2000). *Language, power and pedagogy: Bilingual children in the crossfire*. Buffalo, Multilingual Matters.

Dyson, A., & Genishi, C. (2005). *On the case: Approaches to language and literacy education*. New York, NY: TC Press.

Emerson, R. M., Fretz, R., & Shaw, L. (1995). *Writing ethnographic fieldnotes*. Chicago, IL: The University of Chicago Press.

Erickson, F. (2007). Culture in society and in Educational Practices. In J. A. Banks & C. A. Banks (Eds.), *Multicultural education: Issues and perspectives* (pp. 33–61). New York, NY: John Wiley.

Espenshade, T., & Fu, H. (1997). An analysis of English-language proficiency among U.S. immigrants. *American Sociological Review, 62*, 288–305.

Garcia, G. E. (2003). The reading comprehension development and instruction of English language learners. In A. P. Sweet & C. E. Snow (Eds.) *Rethinking reading comprehension* (pp. 30–50). New York, NY: Guilford.

Gonzalez, N. (2005). Beyond culture: The hybridity of funds of knowledge. In N. Gonzalez, L. N. Moll, & C. Amanti (Eds.), *Funds of knowledge: Theorizing practices in households, communities, and classrooms* (pp. 29–46). Mahwah, NJ: Lawrence Erlbaum.

Harklau, L. (1994). ESL versus mainstream classes: Contrasting L2 learning environments. *TESOL Quarterly, 28*, 241–272.

Ibrahim, A. (1999). Becoming black: Rap and hip hop, race, gender, identity, and the politics of ESL learning. *TESOL Quarterly, 33*, 349–369

Iddings, A. C. D., Risko, V. J., & Rampulla, M. P. (2009). When you don't speak their language: Guiding English-language learners through conversation about text. *The Reading Teacher, 63*, 52–61.

Ladson-Billings, G. (2002). I ain't writin' nuttin': Permission to fail and demands to succeed in urban classrooms. In L. Delpit & J. K. Dowdy (Eds), *The skin that we speak* (pp. 107–120). New York, NY: The New Press.

Ladson-Billings, G. (2007). Culturally relevant teaching: Theory and practice. In J. A. Banks & C. A. Banks (Eds.), *Multicultural education: Issues and perspectives* (pp. 221–245). New York, NY: John Wiley.

Lucas, T., Villegas, A. M., & Freedson-Gonzalez, M. (2008). Linguistically responsive teacher education: Preparing classroom teachers to teach English language learners. *Journal of Teacher Education, 59*, 361–373.

Nieto, S. (2000). *Affirming diversity: The social political context of multicultural education.* Boston, MA: Allyn and Bacon.

Nieto, S. (2002). *Language, culture, and teaching: Critical perspectives for a new century.* Mahwah, NJ: Lawrence Erlbaum.

Ogbu, J. U., & Simons, H. D. (1998). Voluntary and involuntary minorities: A cultural-ecological theory of school performance with some implications for education. *Anthropology and Education Quarterly, 29*, 155–188.

Patton, M. Q. (1990). *Qualitative evaluation and research methods.* Thousand Oaks, CA: Sage.

Portes, A., & McLeod, D. (1996). What shall I call myself? Hispanic identity formation in the second generation. *Ethnic and Racial studies, 16*, 523–547.

Rosenthal, R., & Jacobson, L. (1968). Pygmalion in the classroom. *The Urban Review, 3*, 16–20.

Simmel, G. (2008). The stranger. In P. Kivisto (Eds.), *Social theory: Roots and branches* (pp. 126–129). New York, NY: Oxford University Press.

Sleeter, C. (2005). *Un-standardizing curriculum: Multicultural teaching in the standards-based classroom.* New York, NY: Teachers College Press.

Somé-Guiebré, E. (2011). Tutoring Children of Immigrants in a Multicultural context: A case study. In T. Falola & S. U. Fwatshak (Eds.), *Beyond tradition: African women in cultural and political spaces* (pp. 267–282). Trenton, NJ: Africa World Press.

Valdes, G. (2001). *Learning and not learning English: Latino students in American schools.* New York, NY: Teachers College Press.

Verplaetse, S. L., & Migliacci, N. (2008). Inclusive pedagogy: An introduction. In S. L. Verplaetse & N. Migliacci (Eds), *Inclusive pedagogy for English language learners: A handbook of research-informed practices* (pp. 3–13). New York, NY: Taylor & Francis.

Villenas, S. (2010). The colonizer/colonized Chicana ethnographer. In W. Luttrell (Ed.), *Qualitative educational research: Readings in reflexive methodology and transformative practice* (pp. 345–362). New York, NY: Routledge.

CHAPTER 4

CONCEPTUALIZING SMARTNESS

Using Social and Cultural Capital to Explain Academic Achievement Among a Group of African Immigrant Girls

Betty Okwako

According to distinguished scholars of immigration, Ruben Rumbaut and Alejandros Portes (2001), the U.S. schools have historically been called upon to address societal changes stemming from the arrival of new cultural groups. Rumbaut and Portes (2001) further contend that the diversity of recent immigrants in the U.S. is unprecedented. The current wave of immigration began with the passage of the Immigration Act by the U.S. Congress in 1965 and includes immigrants from Asia, Latin America, the Caribbean, Europe, the Middle East, and Africa (Rumbaut & Portes, 2001). This large-scale immigration has had implications in all aspects of American society, including education. Nearly one in five students in K–12 schooling are children of immigrants (Capps, Fix, Herwantoro, Murray, Ost, & Passel, 2005). Statistics show that while the number of immigrant children has been increasing at a rapid rate at the K–12 level, the highest

Immigration and Schooling: Redefining the 21st Century America, pp. 55–81
Copyright © 2015 by Information Age Publishing
All rights of reproduction in any form reserved.

proportion is enrolled in the upper grades. This trend, add Capps et al. (2005), suggests that high schools face the greatest challenges in educating immigrant children. As a result, numerous studies have been conducted in an attempt to understand the challenges facing immigrant children in school (Conchas, 2006; Qin, 2001; Rumbaut & Portes, 2001).

Despite this interest, we still do not fully comprehend how some immigrant students experience school. This is because research on immigrant education has disproportionately focused on certain immigrant groups. Much of this research has paid attention to Latino and Asian students and focused less on Black immigrants, especially Africans. The few studies that have looked at Black immigrants have mainly attended to the educational experiences of West Indian groups such as Caribbeans, Trinidadians and Jamaicans. In contrast, the schooling experiences of recently arrived African immigrants and refugees remain underresearched. Warinner (2007) goes as far as calling African immigrants the "changing face of immigration" (p. 344) but wonders why scholars have not paid adequate attention to this group. Similarly, not much is known about how African immigrant students navigate the schooling terrain as they try to adapt in their new environments. In this chapter, my premise is that understanding these processes can help educators predict and explain these students' academic outcomes. The findings for this paper were part of a larger study that investigated the educational experiences of one of the least researched immigrant groups in the United States—African immigrant girls in secondary schools. In this chapter, I highlight the relevance of both social and cultural capital in explaining academic outcomes of this group of students.

LITERATURE REVIEW

Participants in the study were characterized by a range of academic abilities, from a high achiever who clearly understood the intricacies of the schooling system to one who was at risk of dropping out of school. I attempt to explain these differences using the social and cultural capital framework (Figure 4.1). I argue that even though these four girls were all immigrants and shared an African heritage, they came from different family backgrounds and social contexts which influenced the ways in which they experienced school, specifically the strategies they used to access resources

Role of Cultural Capital in Education

The term *cultural capital* was coined by Pierre Bourdieu and has been mainly used to explain disparities in education. In trying to understand

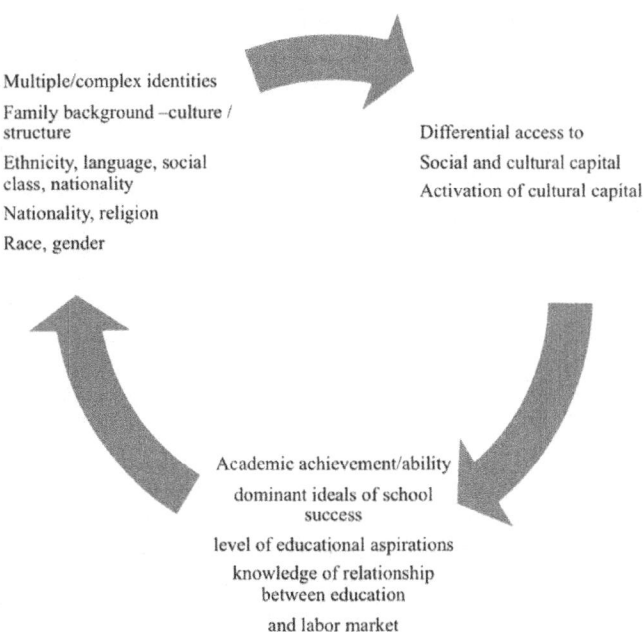

Multiple/complex identities

Family background –culture /
structure

Ethnicity, language, social
class, nationality

Nationality, religion

Race, gender

Differential access to

Social and cultural capital

Activation of cultural capital

Academic achievement/ability

dominant ideals of school
success

level of educational aspirations

knowledge of relationship
between education

and labor market

Figure 4.1.   Social and cultural capital: Explicating variations in educational
outcomes.

the achievement gap between White students and their minority counterparts, scholars have drawn on the notion of cultural capital by arguing that
minority and children from working-class backgrounds lack the valuable
cultural capital for them to succeed in school. From this perspective, the
concepts of social capital and cultural capital were useful in explaining
the resources participants in the study drew upon, to navigate the school
system and how this influenced their academic outcomes. In this sense, I
highlight not just the girls' understanding of schooling procedures, but
also the resources they drew upon in their attempts to achieve academic
success.

According to Bourdieu (1979), while economic disparities are important,
they are not sufficient to explain academic variations between different
groups. Bourdieu and Passeron (1977) have argued that in addition to
economic factors, cultural habits and dispositions inherited from the family
are fundamental for school success. Bourdieu argued that students of the
dominant class are endowed with more valuable social and cultural capital
and as a result, fare better in school than their counterparts who lack such
capital. In this respect, Bourdieu defines *cultural capital* as the general
background, knowledge, and skills that are passed from one generation to

the next. According to Bourdieu, children whose families are of higher economic status inherit more valuable cultural capital than children from the working-class background. Schools, he argues play a big role in the demise of children from lower classes. Macleod (2009) points out, "By embodying class interests and ideologies, schools reward the cultural capital of the dominant classes and devalue that of the lower classes" (p. 14). Dumais (2002) expands on this notion in these terms:

> To acquire cultural capital, students must have the ability to receive and internalize it. Although schools require that students have this ability, they do not provide it for them; rather, the acquisition of cultural capital and the consequent access to academic rewards, depends on the cultural capital passed down by the family, which in turn, is largely dependent on social class. (p. 44)

Lizardo (2010) similarly asserts that cultural capital includes those "resources that are actively mobilized by members of groups or class fractions to establish their difference and to devalue the cultural resources and symbolic practices of outsiders" (p. 310). Consequently, students who do not possess the valued cultural resources are less advantaged academically. These students include racial and ethnic minority students, students from working class backgrounds, and immigrant students.

In her study of a Somali immigrant girl's educational experiences, Bigelow (2008) pointed to the ability to speak English as an important indication of Fadumos' cultural capital. However, the most notable indication of cultural capital was Fadumo's "unwavering belief" in education as the sure path to success in the United States. In addition, Bigelow claims that Fadumo understood the school procedures and was thus able to succeed academically. Fadumo had a perfect attendance record, sought out teachers when she needed help with her work, and always completed her work in time.

Role of Social Capital in Education

Social capital is also viewed in terms of its implications for educational attainment and social mobility. Other prominent scholars, including James Coleman (1987, 1990), have contributed to the development of this theory. Bourdieu was interested in understanding how the middle and the upper middle classes were able to capitalize on material and human resources. Social capital, in this respect, refers to the "resources that inhere in the structure of relations" between individuals and organizations (Costa, 2010, p. 1). The resources are available through a network of relationships. In his study of the educational attainment among children attending private and public schools, Coleman (1998) concluded that children attending private schools fared much better in school because of the strong sense of community and norms that parents, students, and teachers embraced. Coleman further posited that social capital is concerned with how social relationships help children develop their cognitive as well as their social abilities. From this, Coleman concluded that social capital can be beneficial for social mobility of members of low-income and other marginalized communities. Defining social and cultural capital from the above perspectives allows for an analysis of what schools can do to help marginalized students succeed in school (Lubeinski, 2004).

Even though it has been established that different ethnic and cultural groups employ different forms of social capital, White children and third-generation children have been found to possess more valuable social capital than either minority or immigrant children (Bankstone & Zhou, 2002; Kao & Rutherford, 2007; Sun, 1998). For example, Ho and Williams (1996) found that parental participation was significantly higher among Caucasians compared to Hispanics and Asian students. Studies have consistently found that White and some groups of Asian students possess higher levels of social capital compared to minority groups (Coleman, 1988; Stanton-Salazar, 2001; Sun, 1998). According to Lew (2006), the school structure is set up in a way that allows White students easy access to "gatekeepers" who furnish them with important academic and professional resources. Meanwhile poor and minority students struggle in school because of limited access to "institutional gatekeepers" (p. 7).

Ricardo Stanton-Salazar's social network framework was also useful in explaining which relationships the girls in this chapter developed in school and the effects these had as they attempted to succeed in school. From the schooling perspective, Stanton-Salazar (1997, 2001, 2004, 2010) views social capital as "consisting of resources and key forms of social support embedded in one's network or associations and accessible through direct or indirect ties with institutional agents" (p. 117).[1] According to Stanton-Salazar (2004), institutional agents such as teachers and counselors can "manipulate social and institutional conditions in and out of school" and as a result determine which students make it and those who do not (p. 117). Such individuals, adds Stanton-Salazar, serve as gatekeepers and provide access to opportunities that would otherwise be inaccessible to marginalized students. Nieto (1998) similarly contends that such relationships are linked with caring because it is only through trusting and close relationships with teachers that some students will gain access to important schooling resources. While the above theoretical explanations were particularly important in understanding the academic achievements of these four girls, the theoretical explanation that follows was especially pertinent in addressing how these girls constructed their identities based on their day-to-day lived experiences. Since these two concepts were first introduced, numerous scholars of education have attempted to explain the role they play in academic outcomes, yet few of these studies have focused on the educational experiences of immigrant students from Africa. Not much is known about how immigrant children from Africa experience school and how these experiences shape their academic outcomes. This study is an attempt to fill that gap.

METHODS

Participants

Participants for the larger study were purposefully selected (Maxwell, 2005; Miles & Huberman, 1994). They included four African immigrant girls from four different African countries, including Angela, a 16-year-old from Kenya. She accompanied her mother, who came to pursue graduate studies, to the United States. Angela has an older and a younger sister. Belinda is an 18-year-old Congolese girl, who, prior to relocating to the U.S., had moved to Zambia as a result of the Congolese civil war. She comes from a large family. She has three older and three younger siblings. Both her parents work menial jobs. Zura is 18 years old. Her family moved from Sudan ten years ago, due to the Sudanese civil unrest. She is the second child in a family of three. Her mother is an office administrator and her father, a pastor at a local church. Dhahabu is an 18-year-old Burundian girl who was born and raised in a refugee camp in Tanzania. Both her parents work low-wage jobs. Belinda and Dhahabu attend Diversity High[2], a racially diverse urban low-income public school. Zura and Angela attend Dynamo High[3], an equally diverse public school in close proximity to a large Midwestern research university. All the participants except Zura, whose family relocated to the U.S. 10 years ago, have been living in the U.S. for less than four years.

Data Collection Procedures

The methodological approach I took was premised on phenomenological inquiry, a research method that is primarily concerned with understanding the meaning of events and interactions from the participants' perspectives (Bogdan & Biklen, 2005). Given its exploratory and descriptive nature, a phenomenological approach was appropriate for this study as I sought to gain a deeper understanding of the girls' lived experiences. To accomplish this, I employed in-depth phenomenological interviewing (Seidman,

1991), an approach that combines "life history interviewing and in-depth focused interviewing" (p. 15). Life history interviewing allowed me to focus on the girls' personal narratives or stories. According to Seidman (2006), the goal of in-depth interviews is neither to "get answers to questions, nor to test hypothesis, nor to evaluate, but to understand people's lived experiences and the meanings they make from these experiences" (p. 9). Still, Seidman recognizes that even though, as researchers, we can never fully understand participants, we can try to understand their actions. Interviewing, he maintains, allows researchers to appreciate participants' actions and behaviors because they provide contexts for those actions.

Lived experiences, according to Barkley (2009), can only be understood through sharing of stories and memories. Memory making, he adds, is socially influenced—that is, people and places of our lived experiences shape our memories and stories. This study can be viewed as hermeneutic phenomenological research in that it is both descriptive and interpretive (Olafson, 2006; Van Manen, 1990). In the study, I adopted Seidman's (2006) three series interview to avoid what Seidman describes as "treading on thin contextual line" (p. 15). For the interviews, I used open-ended questions with the goal of "building upon and exploring participants' responses to questions" (p. 15). Seidman's three series interview was employed as described below.

The aim of the first series of interviews was to establish the context of the interviewees' experiences. Seidman (2006) refers to this first stage as the *focused life history stage*. Here, the researcher should ask participants to tell him or her as much as they can about their lives in light of the topic under study. In this first stage, I broadly sought to understand participants' range of lived experiences, especially those related to schooling. The second stage of interviewing focused on the *details of experience*. Participants are asked to reconstruct the details of their experiences within the context in which they occur. Here, my goal was to understand participants' present schooling experiences. In this case, I asked them to narrate their day-to-day experiences in school from the time their first class began to the time they went home. Studies such as Conchas (2002) and Stanton-Salazar (2004, 2010), among others, have established the link between minority students' knowledge about school structure and their academic outcomes. Because one of the goals of this study was to understand these girls' academic outcomes, it was necessary that I explore their understanding of the structural aspects of their schools. In the final stage of interviewing, known as *reflection on meaning*, I encouraged my participants to reflect on the meaning the experiences they described held for them. At this final stage of interviewing, participants were required to look at how the different aspects of their lives functioned interactively to lead to their present situation. Seidman adds that this last stage could also take a future orientation.

As such, I asked participants about their educational and career aspirations—what they wanted to do with their lives after school—for example,
if they wanted to go back to their native countries or not.

Data Analysis

I transcribed the interview data myself. Transcription was done immediately after the interviews and was done verbatim. Seidman (2006) posits
that every word that a participant speaks reflects his or her own conscious-
ness. Seidman cautions researchers against substituting participants' words
because to do so is to substitute their consciousness. Data analysis was
ongoing as I collected data (Miles & Huberman, 1984). This approach
helped me develop and ask follow-up questions in subsequent interviews.
I recognize that I have predispositions that might have shaped my transcription and analysis process. Like Laurie Thorpe (2003), my goal was
not to read the transcripts as a set of categories for which I wanted to find
excerpts; rather, the categories arose out of the passages that I marked as
interesting. Participants' responses were then coded manually by marking
each unit of analysis with the emerging coding categories (Bogdan &
Biklen, 2007).

CONCEPTUALIZING SMARTNESS

In this section, I attempt to elucidate girls' perceptions of the opportunity structure in school. How do these perceptions shape their academic
outcomes? I address the above concerns through the analysis of Angela,
Belinda, Dhahabu, and Zura. My goal in this regard is twofold. The first
goal is to elucidate how participants conceptualized achievement. Secondly,
I discuss the strategies they used to achieve academic success. Cultural and
social capital frameworks were helpful in this analysis. I similarly focus on
the notion of academic achievement, a concept participants referred to as
"smartness." Smartness, in this sense, is a relative term used by the girls to
mean success in school. In order to understand how these girls thought of
achievement, I focus on the young women's expectation of schooling and
the processes that led to the fulfillment of these expectations.

In doing this, my goal is to discern the different types of relationships
participants had, not just with their peers, but also with institutional agents
such as teachers, and ultimately how these relationships might have shaped
their educational outcomes. My premise is that the strategies minority
students use to navigate the school terrain and the relationships they form
in the process of doing this, can lead to differential access to institutional

resources necessary for success in school, resulting in differences in academic outcomes. I rely on Stanton-Salazar's (2004) idea that adolescents develop relations with their teachers and peers, which can generate forms of support leading to academic success. Stanton-Salazar further posits that the success of minority students is dependent not only upon "students' level of engagement," but also on "integration in the social and the intellectual fabric of the school" (p. 13).

I begin this section by discussing participants' conceptions of academic achievement. In delineating their accounts of achievement, I compare and contrast these with normative conceptions of achievement, specifically how achievement is defined in schools, by educators, and by society at large. By focusing on this, I demonstrate the influence of cultural capital in the girls' lives in school. Defining achievement in conventional terms demonstrated that, in some ways, they possessed the valued cultural capital necessary for school success. I address how their definitions parallel or differ from not just the conventional views of achievement, but also those of each other.

Next, I address the strategies these girls used to achieve academic success. Participants' narratives suggested that even though they shared views on what it means to be a successful student, they followed different channels to achieve this goal. I address how these girls understood what was expected of them academically and how they responded to these expectations. In addition, they shared some views on how students become smart. Working hard, discipline, motivation, proficiency in English, good teachers, and prior schooling experience were named as requisites for school success. With regard to social capital, I focus on parents' role in helping minority students construct their achievement-oriented identities. Angela's mother, who was a graduate student, stood out in this respect. Angela not only viewed her mother as a role model but also as her advocate in school-related matters. In the final section, I address the girls' understanding of the school's operational procedures. Again, both cultural and social capital frameworks were relevant in this regard. Understanding schooling processes was one indication that these girls understood what was expected of them. I specifically focus on how they utilized the resources and support system available at school and the implication this has on their attempt to succeed. I end the paper by concluding that even though this group of girls shared a common heritage, African and immigrant, they still experienced school differently, leading to differences not only in how they conceptualized achievement, but also in how they defined and constructed their achievement identities.

To address the above points, I draw on the perspectives of all girls, but highlight two of the four participants. In my view, Angela and Dhahabu provide an interesting contrast in terms of achievement. Angela was a high achiever who was excelling in all her classes and understood the intricacies of schooling. In contrast, Dhahabu, who was failing most of her subjects, was once at risk of dropping out of school and lacked clarity on how the school system worked. It can be argued that Angela possessed the valued cultural capital, while Dhahabu did not.

Synopsis of the Girls' Academic Background

Participants' narratives revealed a variety of "cultural selves" or what Lee-Yok (2009) refers to as "subjectivities."[4] The four girls were good and obedient students; except for Belinda, they had both male and female friends from different parts of the world; some were athletes; they were staunch Christians; they complained about their parents and siblings; they had career ambitions, but above, all they wanted to be successful in school even though their view of what success meant sometimes differed (see Table 4.1).

Based on conventional measures of performance, I concluded that, because of her 3.9 GPA, Angela was the most proficient academically of the four girls. Angela also demonstrates the highest level of both cultural and social capital. Even with a GPA of 3.9, she was not satisfied and was aiming for a 4.0 by the time she graduated. As an 11th grader, Angela was in no hurry to decide her future career, though she alluded to "a job in the field of science, such as engineering or architecture." Her career choice fit her academic abilities. Angela performed excellently in math and science, which were also her favorite subjects. Unlike Angela, Zura was an "average" student, who recognized that she could do better in her studies "if only she puts more effort in her work." She was also good at math and wanted to be a high school teacher. Her desire was to work with special needs children. Belinda from Diversity High also referred to herself as an "average" student even though in her last year before she graduated from high school, she had failed three of her subjects. Dhahabu was the least successful academically, and also the one who demonstrated the lowest levels of cultural and social capital. At the time of the study, she was in 12th grade and had failed almost all her subjects the year before.

Regardless of the variations, for the most part, all the girls held positive opinions about school. Similarly, even though they were not all "successful" students, they still wanted to do well in school and, thus, attempted to construct achievement-oriented selves. The strategies they used to accomplish this were contingent upon various factors, including family background, immigration history, and the school environment.

Drawing on Normative Conceptions of School Success

Achievement indicators used by schools include a number of cognitive and noncognitive measures. Like other aspects of schooling, participants'

Table 4.1. Summary of the Girls' Academic Background

Participant	Angela	Zura	Belinda	Dhahabu
Grade	11	12	12	12
GPA as reported by the girls	3.9	2.5	Does not know	Does not know
Duration of stay in the U.S (# of years)	4	10	3	4
GPA that indicates "smartness"	3.75	3.5	3.0	No numeric concept A and B
Favorite subject	Math	Math	Social Studies	Math
School	Dynamo High	Dynamo High	Diversity High	Diversity High
Prior schooling in native country	Elite boarding school	Arabic speaking school	Urban school	Informal schooling at a refugee camp

views regarding achievement sometimes aligned with, but also diverged from the conventional definitions of achievement. While they acknowledged conventional measures of success in school, participants also imposed their own definitions of school success. For instance, they all mentioned GPA, completion of homework, and class participation, but they also pointed to noncognitive aspects of achievement such as level of engagement, discipline, effort, determination, and resilience as important indicators of academic success. This view echoes the critics of the standards movement, including Gloria Ladson-Billings, Geneva Gay, Sonia Nieto among others, who maintain that evidence of success in school should not be restricted to indicators such as standardized scores and GPA. They have called for less emphasis on high-stakes accountability and grades and suggested that noncognitive measures should also be considered when gauging student performance.

As I mentioned earlier, of the four girls, Angela exemplified high achievement in school. In Angela's view, attaining and maintaining a good GPA was important because of her future academic aspirations. Even though she was just an 11th grader, Angela could clearly articulate her future career and academic goals. She wanted to go to college once she graduated from high school, and not just any college; she would "only settle for a big university." Angela was also well aware that a "good GPA is important for admission to a good university." According to her, a good GPA is 3.75 and above. It is not surprising then that when asked what smartness entails, she responded, "A smart person is a person who gets good grades." Achievement in Angela's view is not limited to cognitive skills, though. In a way, she imposes her own definition of smartness by adding, "A smart person is one who also uses common sense in life and does not get in trouble." When I asked her to clarify what she meant by "common sense," she replied:

> When you are told not to do something, you don't do it. Like if you are told something is going to have consequences and you go ahead and do it, then you are not smart. That means they don't use their common sense. Like if a student gets in trouble for obvious stuff. Like some people don't even take school seriously and they don't even care about school. Like those are stupid people. Like they just do whatever in school and they know they will get in trouble.

From this excerpt, Angela certainly draws on "socially sanctioned cultural capital" (Macleod, 2010, p. 423). Angela viewed GPA as the basis of academic achievement but pointed to adherence to school rules and regulations as additional attributes of a successful student. In this sense, Rosen and colleagues (2010) posit that noncognitive traits, such as those mentioned by Angela, can complement effort, leading to better academic outcomes. Even though Angela was a successful student based on normative conceptions of achievement, she still questioned the validity of relying solely on grades as a measure of academic success and suggested that nonacademic attributes should also be included as measures of achievement. Angela was not the only one who expressed this view. Belinda, Dhahabu, and Zura made similar remarks. According to Angela, other indicators of success include exclusive and coveted membership to various organizations such as the National Honor Society (NHS), which students can only join if they have a high GPA, and admission to advanced placement (AP) classes, accomplishments that she has already been achieving. In addition, Angela received a certificate of merit for her exemplary performance when she first attained the 3.75 GPA.

Angela's peer from Dynamo High, Zura, shared her views regarding achievement. She agreed that GPA was an important gauge of academic performance, but when asked what she considered a good GPA, she assigned a lower numeric value of 3.5. Surprisingly, while she averaged an A in math, her cumulative grade point average was only 2.5. She scored excellent grades in math but was performing dismally in other content areas, thus, lowering her GPA. When asked to explain the inconsistency in her grades, she responded: "You can't be gifted equally in all subjects." Given her experiences, Zura believed that academic capabilities vary depending on the subject or class. "Some students are good in math, others in geography, while others are good in music or sports." Zura agreed with Angela that smarts is more than academics. She explained:

> There are some people when you want to have a conversation with them they don't know much about the real world. They just want to talk about books the whole time and about homework. They usually don't want to speak to anybody, and when stuff come out of their mouth is not normal. They are book smart but always say weird stuff.

She continued, "Smartness is when one does well in school or aces their tests, turn in their homework, have a good attitude in class and if they get a 3.5 and above that."

Angela echoed the above point by saying, "I think there are like two types of smart. Like smart in life and smart in school." For these two girls, "smartness" not only entailed cognitive aspects but also subjective attributes including social relations. In other words, smart students not only perform well in school, but they also know how to relate to other people.

Comparably, Dhahabu appeared to be the least proficient academically. Interestingly, she did not view herself as a failure, even though she was performing below average in most of her subjects. When I asked how she gauged herself in terms of achievement, she responded: "Sometimes I get C's and sometimes E's." Her lack of cultural capital has dire consequences for her academically. Not only is she performing below average (based on the normative standards of achievement), she was, at one point, at risk of failing and dropping out of school. At the time of the interview, Dhahabu was failing most of her classes and had been warned several times that she would not graduate if her grades did not improve. Additionally, she does not seem to understand how the grading system works in her school. When I asked her about her GPA, she had no idea because her "teacher had not informed" her. Interestingly, Belinda, Dhahabu's peer at Diversity High School, gave a similar response when I asked her about her GPA. While she did not place blame on the teacher as Dhahabu did, she explained that she just had not checked her grades. Their responses were a bit surprising because at Diversity High, grades are posted online and are password accessible to all students.

Initially, I was baffled at what seemed like these girls' nonchalance toward grades. It would be easy to conclude that these two girls had no sense of urgency regarding their grades or were embarrassed to share their low grades with me, but the reality could be more complex than that. While not realistic, these girls had future educational and career plans and could articulate them relatively well. The fact that they were failing a majority of their subjects had not inhibited them from having hopes for their future. They both wanted to go to college to pursue careers in the banking industry. In a way, they were realistic about this not becoming a possibility because they had alternative plans in case their primary goals did not materialize. Belinda's back-up career plan was forensic science, while Dhahabu wanted to be a nurse. Although their career choices implied that they did not view themselves as failures, it also speaks to their lack of clarity of college expectations. First, they were both failing in math, a subject that is necessary in banking. Secondly, their second options did not align at all with their first career choices. Forensic science and nursing need a different set of skills than banking. If anything, banking is a math-oriented career while the other two are both science-oriented. In any case, they were failing both subjects. Evidently, both girls lacked the right cultural and social capital, thus limiting their understanding of the relationship between schooling and the job market.

In the above analysis, I delineated the role cultural capital played in how these four girls viewed academic success. These four girls had a complex view of how students become smart, one that recognized several operational views of "smartness." I now turn to social capital and how it might have influenced their current achievement status.

RELATIONSHIP WITH TEACHERS AS
A FORM OF SOCIAL CAPITAL

The relationships and networks these four girls formed significantly influenced how they experienced school. Participants' relationship with their teachers seemed pivotal in influencing their achievement and experiences in school. Still, their accounts depicted varying degrees of interactions. Conchas (2001) found that minority students' success greatly depends upon the level of institutional support in the school. In his study of Latino students, Conchas found that students and teachers interact with and respond to each other in distinct ways. Students, Conchas argued, "became active agents" in creating their own success as they "interacted with the school structure and culture" (p. 71). According to Conchas (2006), interaction with teachers was part of the structural and cultural processes.

The four girls perceived institutional agents including teachers in a variety of ways. Both Angela's and Dhahabu's accounts indicated a close relationship with some of their teachers. Even though Angela did not interact much with her teachers, her confidence in her academic ability mainly emanated from how the teachers viewed her. For one, she was confident of her smartness because her teachers reminded her all the time of how "smart" she was. Her mother was also aware of the teachers' positive views of her daughter's academic ability, because "teachers mention this to her all the time when she goes for parents' conferences." Angela admits that she was more engaged in classes with the teachers she liked. She explained, "Usually I am very quiet, but I like geometry and I like the teacher so I talk a lot in that class. I am kind of really good at algebra, so I am also kind of loud too. In French class, I talk a lot too because I like the teacher. English I am like kind of quiet but in science I participate too." Angela said that if she was "too quiet in class" the teacher might not notice her much. She explained:

> I am usually like really quiet, so teachers don't treat me differently. Some classes I am really quiet and some I help people a lot and I am allowed to by the teacher, so it just depends with the class. Some teachers talk to me and some don't. Some say hi and bye when they meet me in the hallway but not like have a conversation.

From the above excerpt we glean that Angela was not concerned that the teacher did not pay attention to her. She did not believe that the teacher was ignoring her, either. Rather, she interpreted the lack of attention as being a result of her passiveness in class. Additionally, the fact that other students always turned to her for help in math class was confirmation in her view that the teacher was aware of her. Knowing this helped reinforce confidence in her academic capabilities.

Like Angela, Dhahabu did not interact much with her teachers. The only school personnel she had any meaningful relationship with seemed to be the ESL staff, whom she refers to as Mrs. Lorenzo. Even then, there were indications that Dhahabu did not fully comprehend Mrs. Lorenzo's role in school, but she knew that she and other students like her could rely on Mrs. Lorenzo whenever they needed assistance in school. Mrs. Lorenzo appeared to be a resource person for English language learners. In the following excerpt, Dhahabu provides a glimpse of what Mrs. Lorenzo's role might be at Diversity High: "I talk to Mrs. Lorenzo though we can talk to any other teacher but I prefer to talk to Mrs. Lorenzo because she is very helpful. She will offer to take you to the office and also help you with learning English."

Still, Dhahabu was not sure whether Mrs. Lorenzo is a teacher or not. She tried to explain Mrs. Lorenzo's role:

> I don't know if she is a teacher but I think she just helps us. I see her take things to the office. Like when there is an exam she takes them from the office. Whenever I have a problem, I can also talk to a teacher who then will tell Miss Lorenzo my problem. If I need help with my work, I will talk to Miss Lorenzo to help me.

From Dhahabu's account, I could not discern the role Mrs. Lorenzo played at Diversity High. Her description of Mrs. Lorenzo is further evidence of Dhahabu's lack of clarity of the schooling processes.

Good Teachers

Participants' interaction with teachers also depended on how much they liked the teachers, the classes, and their capabilities in those classes. For instance, Zura interacted more with the teachers she liked:

> There are some teachers that I like better than others of course. I love my science teacher because he is really nice and he always says hi when you meet him. He is nice to everybody. I think all my teachers are nice too, they just don't say much. But above all teachers my math teacher, I think she likes me more because she is always like "You can do this," "You do not have to do this," and she is always telling us stuff. I talk to her more than other teachers. I am not scared to ask her questions if I don't understand something.

According to Zura, good teachers continuously encourage their students to achieve their potential.

In Belinda's case, she interacted more with the teacher of her "favorite" subject, social studies. She stated:

> I do talk with every teacher but there are some specific teachers I talk to more. But for some teachers I just feel lazy and I feel I know the stuff but when I want to know some specific stuff that is when I ask more like my favorite subject social studies, I ask more questions than other subjects.

She admits that she does not take much interest in teachers except her social studies teacher. Her interest in the subject encourages her to interact with the teacher.

These narratives, as well as those of Angela and Dhahabu, suggested that they interacted more with their "favorite" teachers. When asked why they liked the teachers, they responded similarly that these were the "good" teachers. Good teachers in the girls' opinion were the teachers who were approachable and "easy to talk to." Zura explained her views:

> Good can mean many things because some teachers can be nice just because they have to. Good teachers take time to try and make you learn something. They have patience with you if you do not understand a lesson or something. They will remind you to turn in things if you forgot. They will help you if you need anything. I just think it is nice of them to do that. Plus they genuinely want you to learn.

In Zura's opinion, her chemistry teacher exemplified a good teacher:

> My chemistry teacher is a good teacher. She explains things to you and if you do not understand, she gives us like half an hour after class and she sits at her desk so that if anybody wants help or something she tells us to go to her

because she says she understands that some people are shy to ask question out loudly. She says, "If you have any questions come to me, and sometimes." She stays like two hours after school if people want to see her. As long someone wants to see her, she will stay, however long it takes.

Dhahabu supported the above view:

You see like if a teacher gives us work and then he or she sees that I am struggling with it and when I ask for the help they say "do it yourself," I can say that is not a good teacher. But if I say I need help and the teacher says, "Come, I can help you" then I will say that is a good teacher. Then I will wait [until] he helps me. The teacher can ask me what I am doing after school then if I say nothing, he will say "come after school." But if they say "No after school and no help," then I can say that is not a good teacher. I can't say a teacher has ever said no when I asked them for help. All of my teachers are always willing to help me. Also a teacher who talks to me every day and says hi to me, that's a good teacher too. My math teacher, I asked her "If the test comes and I do not know how to do it, will you help me?" Then he said, "I will help you." And true to his word he was very helpful to me on the day of the exam.

Participants agreed that most of their teachers were "good." Good teachers, in the girls' view, are teachers who care for their students, are always there for them, and acknowledge their presence by greeting them when they encounter students outside of the classroom. They viewed good teachers as the ones who go out of their way to be helpful to students.

Knowledge of School Operational Structures and School Success

How did the four girls understand the *institutional processes* that can shape achievement? If they understood them well, how did they navigate these processes? How did these influence or shape the ways in which they constructed their achievement-oriented selves? Conchas (2006) contends that minority students' understanding of institutional mechanisms in school can lead to academic success. *Institutional processes,* in this case, refer to schooling procedures and policies, including the support system available to students, that help them succeed. I argue that understanding the operational structures (which was an indication of cultural capital) allowed the girls to take advantage of the support system and the opportunities available leading to success in school. In a way, cultural capital mediated social capital in the girls' attempt to navigate school. Participants' narratives demonstrated variations in the ways in which they understood school policies and procedures. I argue that these differences might have influenced the girls' academic outcomes. In this respect, while the four girls expected to succeed in school, the two participants from Dynamo High School had a better understanding of how to navigate the schooling system to attain educational success. On the other hand, the two girls from Diversity High School were not as conversant with these institutional processes.

Stanton-Salazar (1997) posits that for racial and ethnic minority students, school success has never been" simply a matter of learning and competently performing technical skills"; rather, and more fundamentally, "it has been a matter of learning how to decode the system" (p. 13). Reproduction theorists posit that students who possess the dominant cultural capital are able to navigate the system and thus attain success in school. Of the four girls, Dhahabu appeared to be the least informed about how to navigate the schooling system, while Angela seemed to be the savviest in this respect.

As a high achiever, Angela possessed the cultural capital to successfully navigate the school system. She understood the importance of extracurricular activities, such as sports, for her future educational plans. Angela attempted to construct an "athletic" identity, even though she was not good at sports. She first attempted soccer and failed, then she tried track and did not make it on this school team either. Sports, she complained, "just took too much time away from studying." In the end, Angela realized she was "not good at all" at sports and was "wasting time" trying to be an athlete. She complained that she invested such a big proportion of her time practicing sports that it was beginning to interfere with her studies. Despite the time and effort that Angela put into track, her athletic skills did not improve. Angela tried her hand at an "easier" extracurricular activity by joining the African Students Association and serving as the club's president. Even though attempting sports was part of her future educational plans, she gave it up as her extracurricular activity and joined a nonsporting activity, which she claimed "does not take much time" but still served the same purpose. According to Angela, she engaged in these extracurricular activities in preparation for college. This point demonstrates her knowledge of the school culture and structure.

Extracurricular activities are not just important for future educational possibilities. Studies on youth networks such as Hanks and Eckland (1976) have established that extracurricular activities can be avenues for peer acceptance and an additional source of social capital for young people. According to Hanks and Eckland, extracurricular activities not only help foster academic success via social networks, but they also facilitate self-esteem and self-confidence. Angela was a perfect example of this. In addition to sports, Angela was a member of the National Honor Society and was the president of the African Students Association, a position that speaks highly of her leadership qualities. When I asked how she ended up in that position, she replied that her teachers nominated her. Again, this demonstrates the relationship she had with her teachers.

In contrast, Dhahabu appeared not to have a clear understanding of what school policies meant and the implication this would have on her future plans, academic or otherwise. For instance, at the beginning of the semester the study took place, she still had no information of what her GPA was, yet she made no effort to try and find out why the school had not revealed this to her. Still, not knowing her grade was not just a simple case of recklessness or not caring for education. I have established that Dhahabu cared for school and wanted to succeed. In my view, this could have been her strategy of resisting dominant ideals of success. Additionally, even though she declared her intention of going to college, she had no plan or strategy in place of how she would get there. Again, this demonstrated lack of understanding the intricacies of college preparation. For one, she was not and had never been involved in any extracurricular activity at her school. She did not play any sports or belong to any club, and, most importantly, there was no indication of meaningful relationships with institutional agents other than her ESL teacher.

Dhahabu was aware that some of her teachers expected the least from her. For instance, while emphasizing the importance of passing her math class, the teacher informed her that graduating from school hinged on whether she would make it in that class. Dhahabu complained that it seemed to her as if the teacher expected her to fail the class. Her teacher explained that if she failed the class, she would have to drop out of school. Passing the math class was therefore crucial to Dhahabu, yet Dhahabu admitted that she never once approached her teacher for help. She seemed resigned and accepting of what she saw as inevitable—failing the class and eventually dropping out of school.

Dhahabu explained the repercussions of failing the class, but it was clear that she did not understand the policy. Still, Dhahabu was worried that, like her older siblings, she might not be able to complete high school. However, it would be too simplistic to assume that Dhahabu is not concerned about her prospects of not finishing school.

At the same time, Dhahabu's limited knowledge of how the system operated does not mean that she could not notice structural flaws. This was evident when I asked how she felt when she was informed that she might not graduate. She explained:

> You know so many people have intervened and tried to speak for me, but that's just the policy. They say that once your age reaches 18 you should just leave. The teachers say they have no control over that. But I think these people are very smart because they remove you very slowly without you being aware of what is going on. Before you know it, it is time to go. When you

ask them why this is happening, some tell you it is "a job that someone has to do." It is not their wish to do this … it is a government's rule. For them it is a job … just a job.

Even though not critical of the system, Dhahabu is still aware of the injustices that she and other immigrant students face in school. She sees these injustices even though she does not actively challenge what other people say or seek outside help. But she still holds on and works, hoping to reach her goal of graduating from high school.

PARENTS' ROLE AS FORMS OF
CULTURAL AND SOCIAL CAPITAL

Parents played an important role in shaping these participants' academic identities. Angela's mother particularly stood out in this respect. For instance, on the bumper of her car, she had a sticker reading "My child is an honors student." This speaks to her pride regarding Angela's academic accomplishments. Like Angela, her mother was equally proud of her "honors student" label and helped to validate it. Angela's family background provided her with the necessary tools to succeed in school. Lareau (1987) provides insights into the relationship between family background and educational outcomes. She argues that while there are different factors that could affect family–school relations, and the degree of relations, she agrees there is a dominant type of relationship. According to Lareau (1987), in this type of relationship, parents are not only involved in the curricular aspects of schooling, but they also play an active role in the formal aspects of their children's cognitive development.

In explaining the role of social capital to educational and life outcomes, Coleman (1987) similarly notes that parents' level of education can positively influence their children's schooling outcome. However, parents' level of education is not sufficient for children to succeed in school. He added that in the absence of a meaningful relationship with their children, a high level of education will be irrelevant in the educational growth of their children. As a graduate student, Angela's mother understood this and provided her with the necessary support Angela needed to succeed in school. On numerous occasions, I found Angela and her mother discussing homework. I also witnessed her offering her academic-related guidance, such as providing suggestions on which classes to enroll in at the beginning of the semester.

This is a sharp contrast from Dhahabu's case, in which no amount of intervention from her parents would change her situation when they tried to advocate for their daughter to be placed in the right grade. In fact, Mr.

Kabila, Dhahabu's father, informed me how frustrated he was with the school when he was trying to address his daughter's situation. When the school decided to place Dhahabu five grades higher than where she should have been, her father attempted on several occasions to intervene, but to no avail. He went to the school several times and spoke to the teachers, trying to convince them to rethink the decision, but the school ignored him. Given Dhahabu's limited English and academic skills, Mr. Kabila felt it would not serve Dhahabu well to be promoted five grades.

Lareau's (1987) argument is pertinent in understanding the differences in the ways Angela and Dhahabu's parents helped shape their daughters' academic selves. Angela's mother is also a former teacher. She therefore had knowledge of how the school system works and how she could advocate for her daughter. On several occasions, she has advocated for her daughter to be enrolled in AP classes. On the other hand, Dhahabu's parents could neither speak nor write in English. Clearly, Dhahabu's parents did not possess the social and cultural capital that can "facilitate their compliance with the dominant standards in school interactions" (Lareau, 1992, p. 42). In addition to their refugee status, Dhahabu's parents had to deal with a significant language barrier while negotiating various relationships in school. They were also worried that their third child would have to drop out of school for being over the legal age for school. When I asked Dhahabu what her parents were doing about this, she stated that like her, they felt powerless to do anything. Her parents believed that the school set their daughter up for failure when they placed her five grades above where they felt she should have been.

CONCLUSION AND IMPLICATIONS FOR
TEACHING AND LEARNING

Bartolome and Trueba (2000) contend that true democracy entails real commitment to educating immigrants and other minorities in this society. How do educators stay true to this commitment? They can address this by showing genuine care and concern for all children. This begins with understanding why this group of students experience school in the way they do. Understanding the networks these students form in school is a good place to begin. Participants' accounts suggest that having a sense of belonging is important to students from backgrounds such as theirs. Yet we see how Dhahabu and Belinda are alienated in many ways. These two girls who were the least achievers of the four did not engage in any kind of after-school activities, and neither did they interact much with their peers or teachers at school. Not having meaningful relationships with teachers and peers meant that the two girls lacked the opportunity to develop the cultural and social capital that is necessary for school success. On the other hand, Angela and Zura, who were very active and more successful academically, spoke of meaningful relationships with peers and teachers, were engaged in different clubs and sports, and could articulate not only their future educational and career goals but also how to realistically achieve those goals.

This study also reminds us of the power of cultural capital. Cultural capital was particularly significant as it informed the ways in which the four girls attempted (or not) to access and develop networks in school. Furthermore, their ideas of school success were shaped not only by their knowledge, but also how they used or tried to access the opportunities available for them to succeed in school. My findings suggest that the ways in which these girls positioned themselves supported and constrained their access to both cultural and social capital. For instance, Zura and Angela, the two academically proficient students, were very involved within the mainstream life in their school. They participated in school activities, had friends—American and non-American—and they embraced many of the mainstream norms of schooling.

On the other hand, the lack of social and cultural capital was manifested in the girls' accounts in various ways, particularly for the girls at Diversity High. They demonstrated limited knowledge in the ways the school operated. Dhahabu had no understanding of the graduation policy, even though this had a dire impact on her scholastic achievement. Through the career choices they articulated, it was also clear that the two girls lacked an understanding of the relationship between schooling and the labor market. Even though both were failing in math, an important requisite for careers in banking, both wanted careers in that industry. In addition, while it is important to note that the two girls had alternative career paths in case banking does not materialize, there was a mismatch in their two plans.

CONCLUSION

This chapter is premised on the fact that participants possessed varying degrees of social and cultural capital. This was reflected in the strategies they used to navigate the school system. Their accounts suggest the two girls from Dynamo High were more knowledgeable of the operational structure of the school and were clearly taking advantage of the resources available to make them better students. Angela, who best understood the intricacies of the system, reaped the most benefit out of it. Again, it is not surprising that of the four participants, she was the most academically successful. On the other hand, Dhahabu, who was struggling the most academically, seemed to lack the necessary social and cultural capital to successfully maneuver the school system. She seemed to have the least understanding of school expectations, had no meaningful relationships with either her teachers or peers, and was not involved in any extracurricular activities.

REFERENCES

Agar, M. (1995). *The professional stranger: An informal introduction to ethnography*. San Diego, CA: Academic Press.

Anyon, J. (1981). Social class and school knowledge. *Curriculum Inquiry, 11*(1), 3–42.

Apple, M. (1992). Education, culture and class power: Basil Bernstein and the Neo-Marxist sociology of education. *Educational Theory, 42*(2), 127–145.

Banks, J., & Banks C.M, (2010). *Multicultural education: Issues and perspectives*. Hoboken, NJ: John Wiley & Sons.

Bigelow, H. M. (2007). *Social and cultural capital: The case of a Somali teenage girl*. Richmond, VA: Literacy Institute at Virginia Commonwealth University.

Bogdan, B. C., & Bilken, S. K. (2007). *Qualitative research for education: An introduction to theories and methods*. Boston, MA: Pearson.

Bourdieu, P. (1977). Cultural reproduction and social reproduction. In J. Karabel & A.S. Halsey, (Eds.), *Power and ideology in education* (pp. 487–511). New York, NY: Oxford University Press.

Bourdieu, P., & Passseron, J. C. (1977). *Reproduction in education, society and culture*. Thousand Oaks, CA: Sage.

Bowles, S., & Gintis, H. (1976). *Schooling in capitalist America: Educational reform and the contradictions of economic life*. New York, NY: Basic Books.

Carter, P., & Wairakoo, N. (2009). Cultural explanations for racial and ethnic stratifications in academic achievement: A call for a new and improved theory. *Review of Educational Research, 79*(1), 366–395.

Capps, R. Fix, M., Herwantoro, Murray, J., Ost, J. & Passel, J. S. (2005). *The new demographics of American schools: Immigration and the No Child Left Behind Act*. Washington, DC: The Urban Institute.

Chavous, T., Hilkerne-Benart, D., Schmeelk-Cone, K., Caldwell, C., Kone-Wood, L., & Zimmermann, M. (2003). Racial identity and academic attainment among African American adolescents. *Child Development, 74*(4), 1076–1090.

Cokley, K., & Chapman, C. (2008). The roles of ethnic identity, anti-White attitudes and academic self-concepts in African-American student achievement. *Social Psychology of Education, 11*(4), 349–365.

Coleman, J. S. (1987). Social capital and the development of youth. *Momentum, 18*(4), 6–8.

Coleman, J. S. (1990). *Foundations of social theory*. Cambridge, MA: The Belknap Press of Harvard University Press.

Conchas, G. (2002). *The color of success: Race and high achieving urban youth*. New York, NY: Teachers College.

Cotterell, J. (1996). *Social networks and social influences in adolescence*. New York, NY: Routledge

Creswell, J. W. (1988). *Qualitative inquiry and research design: Choosing among the five traditions.* Thousand Oaks, CA: Sage.

Cross, W. E. (1991). *Shades of black: Identity in African American identity.* Philadelphia, PA: Temple University Press.

Cunningham, E. G., Wang, C., & Bishop, N. (2000). *Challenges to school engagement and school effectiveness indicators.* Melbourne, Australia: Swinburne University of Technology. Retrieved from http://www.shs-wasc.info/feelingsaboutschool

Dumais, S. (2002). Cultural capital, gender and school success: The role of habitus. *Sociology of Education, 75*(1), 44–68.

Erkut, S., Fields, J. P., Sing, R., & Marx, F. (2002). *Diversity in girls' experiences: Feeling good about who you are.* San Francisco, CA: Jossey-Bass.

Everett, C. (2010). "Precious" star Gabourey Sidibe opens up about being snubbed in *Vanity Fair*'s Young Hollywood. *New York Daily News.* Retrieved from http://www.nydailynews.com/gossip

Faliciano, C., & Rumbaut, R. (2005). Gendered paths: Educational and occupational expectations and outcomes among adult children of immigrants. *Ethnic and Racial Studies, 28*(6), 1087–1118.

Falola, T., & Afolabi, N. (2007). *The human cost of African immigration.* New York, NY: Routledge.

Ferguson, A. (2000). *Bad boys: Public schools and the making of black masculinity.* Ann Arbor, MI: University of Michigan Press.

Fordham, S. (2003). These loud Black girls: (Black) women silence and gender passing in the academy. *Anthropology in Education, 24*(1), 3–32.

Gibson, M. (1991). Ethnicity, gender and social class: The school adaptation patterns of West Indian youths. In M. Gibson & J. Ogbu (Eds.), *Minority status and schooling: A comparative study of immigrant and involuntary minorities.* New York, NY: Garland.

Giddens, A. (1984). *The constitution of the society: Outline of the theory of structuration.* Cambridge, UK: Polity Press.

Goffman, E. (1959). *The presentation of self in everyday life.* New York, NY: Doubleday.

Hewstone, M., & Brown, P. (1986). Contact is not enough: An intergroup perspective on the Contact hypothesis. In M. Hewstone & P. Brown (Eds.), *Contact and conflicts in intergroup encounters* (pp. 1–44). New York, NY: Blackwell.

Hill-Collins, P. (1991). *Black feminist thought.* New York, NY: Routeldge.

Holland, D., Lachiotte, W., Skinner, D., & Cain, C. (1998). *Identity and agency in cultural worlds.* Cambridge, MA: Harvard University Press.

Kelly, U. (1997). *Schooling desire: Literacy, cultural politics, and pedagogy.* New York, NY: Routledge.

Kunz, J., & Hanvey, L. (2000). *Immigrant youth in Canada.* Kanata, ON: Canadian Council on Social Development.

Lamont, M. (1992). *Money, moral and manners: The culture of the French and American upper-middle class.* Chicago, IL: University of Chicago Press.

Lamont, M. (2000). *The dignity of working men: Morality and the boundaries of class, race and immigration.* New York, NY: Russell Sage Foundation.

Lee, S. (1997). The road to college: Hmong American women's pursuit of higher education. *Harvard Educational Review, 67*, 803–826.

Lee, S. J. (2001). Exploring and transforming the landscape of gender and sexuality: Hmong American teenage girls. *Race, Gender & Class, 8*(1), 35–46.

Lew, J. (2006). *Asian Americans in class: Charting the achievement gap among Korean American youth*. New York, NY: Teachers College Press.

Lizardo, O. (2010). Individuals and groups: Identity and performance. In J. R. Hall, L. Grindstaf, & M. C. Lo (Eds.), *Handbook of cultural sociology*. New York, NY: Routledge.

Lubienski, S. T. (2003). Celebrating diversity and denying disparities: A critical assessment. *Educational Researcher, 32*(8), 30–38.

Macleod, J. (1995). *Ain't no making it: Aspirations and attainment in a low-income neighborhood*. San Francisco, CA: Westview Press.

Marshall, C., & Rossman, G. (1995). *Designing qualitative research*. London, UK: Sage.

Merten, D. E. (1997). The meaning of meanness: Popularity and completion among junior high school girls. *Sociology of Education, 70*, 175–191.

Michigan Department of Education. (n.d.). Retrieved from http://www.michigan.gov/mde

Miles, M. B., & Huberman, M. A. (1994). *Qualitative data analysis*. London, UK: Sage.

Ngo, B. (2010). *Unresolved identities: Discourse, ambivalence and urban immigrant student*. Albany, NY: State University of New York Press.

Nieto, S. (1992). *Affirming diversity: The sociopolitical context of multicultural education*. New York, NY: Longman.

Ogbu, J. (1978). *Minority education and caste: The American system in cross-cultural perspective*. New York, NY: Academic Press.

Ogbu, J. (1982). Cultural discontinuities and schooling. *Anthropology and Education Quarterly, 13*(4), 290–307.

Ogbu, J. (1983). Minority status and schooling in plural societies. *Comparative Education Review, 27*(2), 168–190.

Olafson, L. (2006). *It's just easier not to go to school: Adolescent girls and disengagement in middle school*. New York, NY: Peter Lang.

Phelan, P., Davidson, A. L., & Cao, H. T., (1991). Students' multiple worlds: Negotiating the boundaries of family, peer, and school cultures. *Anthropology & Education Quarterly, 22*(3), 224-250.

Portes, A., & Rumbaut, R. G. (2001). *Legacies: The story of the immigrant second generation*. Berkeley, CA: University of California Press.

Qin-Hilliard, D. B. (2006). The role of gender in immigrant children's educational adaptation. *Current Issues in Comparative Education, 9*(1), 8–19.

Qin-Hilliard, D. B. (2003). Gendered expectations and gendered experiences: Immigrant students' adaptation in school. *New Directions in Youth Development Special Issue: The Social Worlds of Immigrant Youth, 100*, 91–110.

Reinharz, S. (1992). *Feminist methods in social Science research*. New York, NY: Oxford University Press.

Rong, X. L., & Brown, F. (2001). The effects of immigrant generation and ethnicity on educational attainment among young African and Caribbean Blacks in the United States. *Harvard Educational Review, 71*(3), 536–565.

Rosaldo, R. (1993). *Culture and truth: The remaking of social analysis*. Boston, MA: Beacon Press.

Rumbaut, R., & Portes, A. (2001). *Ethnicities: Children of immigrants in America*. New York, NY: Russell Sage Foundation.

Saroub, L. (2005). *All American Yemeni girls: Being Muslim in a public school*. Philadelphia, PA: University of Pennsylvania Press.

Seidman, I. (2006). *Interviewing as a qualitative research: A guide for researchers in education and the social Sciences*. New York, NY: Teachers College Press.

Sellers, R. M., & Shelton, J. N. (2003). The role of racial identity in perceived racial discrimination. *Journal of Personality and Social Psychology, 84*(5), 1079–1092.

Stanton-Salazar, R. (1997). A social capital framework for understanding the socialization of racial minority children and youths. *Harvard Educational Review, 67*(1), 1–40.

Stanton-Salazar, R., & Donbursch, S. M. (1995). Social capital and the reproduction of inequality: The transformation of informational networks among Mexican-origin high school students. *Sociology of Education, 68*(2), 116–135.

Suarez-Orozco, C., & Suarez-Orozco, M. (2001). *Children of immigration*. Cambridge, MA: Harvard University Press.

Tatum, B. Teaching for Change. *Harvard Educational Review*. Cambridge, MA.

Takougang, J., & Tidjani, B. (2009). Settlement patterns and organizations among African immigrants in the United States. *Journal of Third World Studies, 26*(1), 31–40.

Terrazas, A. (2009). *African immigrants in the United States*. Migration Policy Institute. Retrieved from http://www.migrationinformation.org/usfocus

Toren, N. (2001). Women and immigrants: Strangers in a strange land. In R. J., Simon (Ed.), *Immigrant women* (pp.?). New Brunswick, NJ: Transactions.

Trueba, E. T., & Bartolome, L. I. (2000). *Immigrant voices: In search of educational equity*. Lanham, MD: Rowman & Littlefield.

U. S. Bureau of the Census. (2000). *Current population reports*. Washington DC: Department of Commerce, Economics and Statistics Administration.

Valenzuela, A. (1999). *Subtractive schooling: U.S.–Mexican youth and the politics of caring*. New York, NY: State University of New York.

Valenzuela, A. (2009). Social justice by caring. University of Chicago Commencement Speech.

Van Manen, M. (1990). *Researching lived experiences: Human science for an action sensitive pedagogy*. London, UK: The Althouse.

Vasquez, J. (2010). Blurred borders for some but not "Others": Racialization, flexible Ethnicity, gender and the third generation Mexican-American Identity. *Sociological Perspectives, 58*(1), 45–71.

Vickerman, M. (1999). *Crosscurrents: West Indian immigrants and race*. Oxford, UK: Oxford University Press.

Warikoo, N. K., (2010). Symbolic boundaries and structure in New York and London schools. *American Journal of Education, 116*(3), 423–451.

Warinner, D. (2007). Language, learning and the politics of belonging: Sudanese women refugees, becoming and being "American." *Anthropology and Education Quarterly, 38*(4), 343–359.

Waters, M. (1999). *Black identities: West Indian immigrant dreams and American realities.* Cambridge, MA: Harvard University Press.

Zhou, M., & Kim, S. S. (2006). Community forces, social capital, and educational achievement: The case of supplementary education in the Chinese and Korean immigrant communities. *Harvard Educational Review, 76*(1), 1–29.

PART II

LANGUAGE, MINORITY STUDENTS, AND ACADEMIC ACHIEVEMENT

CHAPTER 5

CHALLENGING A
TROUBLING MISEDUCATION

Arab Americans in
American Schools and Universities

Muna Jamil Shami

INTRODUCTION

Consistent with John Dewey's assertion that democracy is an ideal that we must continually strive toward, Maxine Greene (1995, p. 66) describes democracy as "always in the making." As the democratic experiment begins the 21st century, Henry Giroux (2006) argues that "critical education and the promise of global democracy face a crisis of enormous proportions" (p. 60). Cornel West (2004) also notes that the battle of the century is the "dismantling of empire and the deepening of democracy. This is as much or more a colossal fight over visions and ideas as a catastrophic struggle over profits and missiles" (p. 22).

For Dewey, democracy was a way of life. He believed the aim of education was to prepare and empower students to be active citizens in a participatory

Immigration and Schooling: Redefining the 21st Century America, pp. 85–108
Copyright © 2015 by Information Age Publishing
All rights of reproduction in any form reserved.

democratic society. The Institute for Democratic Education in America (IDEA) defines democratic education as "learning that equips every human being to participate fully in a healthy democracy." This could be achieved by teaching the necessary skills to enable citizens to think critically, reason, justify, and make responsible decisions based on evidence. Dewey viewed democracy as the political manifestation of the scientific method. In his essay *Education as Politics*, Dewey challenged the role of schools in the development of a citizenry that was ill-prepared to participate in a democratic society. He viewed traditional education as formation outside the individual and progressive education as development from within the individual. While critical of other areas of progressive education, he credited it for introducing this important process where traditional education had failed.

Social issues are mirrored in the schools. Since the birth of the common school movement in the 1830s, American public schools have been used as a tool to solve the social issues of the nation (Rury, 2005). If the battle of the day is the deepening of democracy, then schools and universities are the inevitable battlegrounds for competing interests. To deepen democracy, there must be an increase in civic participation and a broadening of political discourse. By broadening democratic spaces, a more effective participatory democracy may emerge, sharing multiple perspectives that reinvigorate the national imagination to move the nation and the world forward together.

Throughout American history, there have always been marginalized groups whose voices were silenced. The shifting demographics of the nation have brought increased diversity and have shone light on the centrality of pluralism in the democratic project. Gates (1992) asserts that the challenge facing America in the next century will be the shaping, at long last, of a truly common public culture, one response to the long-silenced cultures of color. If we relinquish the ideal of America as a plural nation, we abandon the very experiment that America represents—and we renounce the ideals of humanistic education and scholarship inherent in that experiment.

As the nation continues to strive for the democratic ideal, America must rise to the challenge of shaping a common public culture by broadening public spaces and centering freedom and pluralism in democratic dialogue. The ideal plural participatory democracy requires civic engagement by all of its citizens with their multiple narratives and perspectives. Greene (1995) maintains, "All we can do, I believe, is cultivate multiple ways of seeing and multiple dialogues in a world where nothing stays the same" (p. 16).

This chapter examines the experiences of Arab Americans in formal and informal educational settings as a window to the threats facing democratic pluralism in America. Arab Americans, like other underrepresented groups in America, are positioned such that their lived experiences signify the dissonance between the democratic ideal that is the foundation of the nation and America's historical and contemporary policies of oppression—domestic and foreign. Arab Americans have long been active contributors in building the unfinished American democracy. The experiences of the participants in the study may offer insight for schools, universities, and informal educational programs that seek to reinvigorate participatory democracy through critical democratic education.

METHODOLOGY

The data were collected in 2009 as part of the author's dissertation research. The researcher developed a survey to explore Arab Americans' perceptions of how Arabs are socially constructed in America and their lived experiences, including their experiences in formal and informal educational settings. The online survey was completed by 386 Arab Americans. The survey was sent to a purposive sample of self-identified Arab Americans and Arabs who have lived in America for an extended period of time.

Survey respondents were invited to participate, using three primary strategies. A unique URL was programmed for each of the methods to identify the approach that yielded the greatest number of respondents. The first strategy involved sending e-mail invitations to 470 personal contacts asking them to participate in the survey (n=201, 50.1%). The second approach involved asking personal contacts to forward an invitation and link to the survey to their contacts ($n = 108$, 26.9%). The third strategy involved e-mailing the invitation to community listservs of Arab American organizations, student clubs, and Palestine activists ($n = 59$, 14.7%). Community organizations were also contacted and asked to forward the invitation over their listservs to maximize broad participation of Arab Americans.

Self-identification of Arab Americans assumes some degree of connection to an Arab ethnic identity. Only Arab Americans who self-identify as Arabs were captured in the study. Data are missing on Americans who trace their ancestry to Arab countries, yet do not identify as Arab Americans. A major issue faced in studying Arab Americans is that statistical data are not readily available about Arab American students. For the most part, states and school districts do not disaggregate data for Arab American students, and they are typically subsumed as White. Without statistical data readily available, studies of Arab Americans often rely on qualitative methods.

The sampling method skewed the composition of the sample. More than half of the samples are of Arab Americans who trace their national heritage to Palestine. The sample includes more women (59.2%) than men, and almost 40% of participants are from the Washington, DC area. Sixty-three percent of survey respondents were under age 35.[2] This is due to the sampling method, which relied on personal contacts and listservs. The qualitative nature of the data from this exploratory study does not allow for generalizability of the findings beyond the sample that participated in the study, and further research needs to be conducted to determine if the findings hold true for the Arab American population. Instead, the results of this study provide researchers, community members, educators, and cultural workers with information to guide future programs and research studies.

Quantitative and qualitative data analyses were conducted. Survey Monkey was used to filter the survey results to eliminate responses from respondents who were younger than 18 years old from the analysis. Descriptive statistics were initially provided by Survey Monkey, and further analyses were conducted using Microsoft Excel. Survey Monkey was also used to analyze cross-tabs across survey items. The qualitative analysis of the open-ended items from the survey was conducted to analyze emerging themes. The themes were then examined to determine if any of the themes could be combined or if any subthemes emerged.

Description of Sample

The lack of a distinct ethnic demographic category for Arab Americans has resulted in a wide range of estimates regarding the Arab American population. There are an estimated 1.2 to 3.5 million Arab Americans living in America today.[3] The U.S. Census Bureau estimated a 40% increase in the number of Arabs in America in the 1990s (de la Cruz & Brittingham, 2003). The total number of survey respondents ($n = 401$) was reduced as the participants who indicated they were under 18 years of age were eliminated from the sample. The resulting number of survey participants was 386; however, not all of these participants completed the survey. For this reason, the number of participants is reported for each of the questions in the sample description and results section.

Arabs trace their roots back to 22 countries: Algeria, Bahrain, Comoros, Djibouti, Egypt, Iraq, Jordan, Kuwait, Lebanon, Libya, Mauritania, Morocco, Oman, Palestine, Qatar, Saudi Arabia, Somalia, Sudan, Syria, Tunisia, United Arab Emirates, and Yemen (Naber, 2000; Suleiman, 1999). Seventy-five percent of Arabs in America are citizens, and an estimated 46% were born in America (Brittingham & de la Cruz, 2005). Fifty percent of survey respondents were born in America, and 47.0% were born in an Arab country. More than half of the survey respondents (54.3%) have lived in an Arab country, and 38.4% visit routinely. Only 3.1% of respondents reported that they had never visited an Arab country. The survey respondents trace their national heritage back to 15 of the 22 Arab countries.

According to census statistics, the greatest number of Arab-Americans traced their heritage to Lebanon (45.8%), Syria (15.1%), Egypt (9.1%), and Palestine (5.6%).[4] More than half of the respondents are from Palestine (55.5%), and 20.7% of respondents are from Lebanon. Eleven percent of respondents trace their roots to Egypt and 9.7% to Syria. Ten percent of respondents indicated that they are of mixed heritage in that they are both Arab and another ethnicity/race.

There have been three major waves of Arab immigration to America. The initial wave took place between 1870 and World War II, the second wave of immigration was after World War II through the 1960s, and the most recent wave has been since the 1960s (Naber, 2000; Suleiman, 1999). The majority of the early Arab immigrants were Christians from Greater Syria who came to America seeking economic opportunity (Suleiman, 1999). Consistent with the experiences of other immigrant groups of the time, the first wave of Arab Americans assimilated into the dominant culture. This included changing family names to more Americanized names and replacing their native Arabic language with English (Naber, 2000). This disconnection from their Arab identity and community may account for the fact that only 4.1% of survey respondents noted that they or their families immigrated to America in this first wave, and 11.1% of respondents reported that they or their families arrived between 1939 and 1964.

The passage of the Immigration and Nationality Law (Hart-Celler Act) of 1965 eliminated the quota system based on national origin and opened the nation to greater diversity as more immigrants arrived from "non-white nations" (Hochschild & Burch, 2007). Forty-two percent of survey respondents indicated that they or their family immigrated to America between 1965 and 1979. This later wave of immigration also brought a more diverse Arab population to America. They were both Christian and Muslim and came from several Arab countries, often forced out of their countries due to social and political turmoil. The sociopolitical currents of the time and the societal shift in America towards pluralism in the 1960s gave rise to an Arab American identity (Naber, 2000; Suleiman, 1999), which is continuously being negotiated. Twenty-three percent of survey respondents arrived in America in the 1980s, 13.8% in the 1990s, and 5.7% (21 of 370) since 2000.[5]

Survey respondents described the reasons that they or their families migrated to America, including the circumstances in their native country that prompted their departure, the reasons that America became their adopted country, and a description of what was often several steps in between. Consistent with the literature on Arab immigration, the two primary push factors that respondents cited for leaving their native countries were political turmoil/war and lack of economic opportunity. Respondents specifically cited the war and political turmoil in Palestine (displaced by establishment of Israel in 1948, 1967 Israeli occupation, and since the 2000 Al-Aqsa intifada or uprising), Lebanon (1975 civil war, 1982 Israeli invasion and occupation), and Iraq (1990 Gulf War, 2003 Iraq war). Related responses included leaving to escape discrimination, persecution, and repression.

Those who chose to immigrate to America did so because they were seeking security, freedom, and greater opportunity. Respondents mentioned that their families immigrated to America to provide their children with a better life, with the two primary pull factors being greater educational and economic opportunities. Some respondents noted the search for opportunity was driven by the necessity to provide financial support to their families who remained in their countries of origin. For some of the respondents, they or their families did not come to America with the intention of staying permanently but to study or work and then return as the war subsided or as the political situation settled down. While many chose to adopt America as their new home, several respondents left their native countries as refugees. Some noted that they continue to live in exile. Many Palestinian respondents indicated that they have been denied the right to return to their home country.

NARROWING PUBLIC DISCOURSE THREATENING DEMOCRATIC PLURALISM

The vast majority of the participants in the study (83.2%) reported that there is a need to broaden public discourse in America—to reinvigorate democratic dialogue that includes a diversity of perspectives on issues that concern them. The survey respondents rank-ordered Hollywood's movies and television, school classrooms and textbooks, the news media, and university classrooms and course readings as the most constricted spaces of discourse in America.[6] One respondent shared that they were "very concerned by [the] lack of balance, even on public radio."

Of the 83.2% of respondents that indicated the need for alternate perspectives in American public discourse, 13.4% perceive that there are no alternate perspectives represented on the issues of greatest concern to them. Only 11.9% of survey participants perceive that there is some dialogue that includes multiple perspectives on the issues of greatest concern to them, and 4.4% believe there is a healthy amount of dialogue regarding such issues. A respondent commented on the status of public discourse regarding Arabs and issues impacting Arab Americans: "In America there is practically no dialogue in the corporate, for-profit press. The progressive press is less pressured by the money, but still affected by American needs for acculturation [sic], thereby creating an ignorance of language or depth of knowledge of the Arab and Islamic worlds." Another respondent added, "There is not public discourse, only shock jock radio hosts spreading fear and hatred against Arabs and Muslims."

The Internet was ranked as the most open context for sharing a diversity of perspectives, with more than half of respondents (52.8%) indicating that multiple perspectives are presented on the Internet; an additional 30.4% noted that, at least, some alternative perspectives are presented. Cultural and arts spaces (e.g., music/poetry in cafés, art exhibits, film screenings, comedy) followed, with 32.1% finding that multiple perspectives are presented and 46.2% adding that some alternative perspectives are presented. University student clubs were ranked as the third most open space.

According to survey respondents, the three narrowest spaces were Hollywood (movies and television), schools (K–12 classrooms and textbooks), and the news media (television, radio, magazines), in that order. Eighty-nine percent of respondents indicated that mostly or only dominant perspectives are presented by Hollywood. One of the participants said: "I began to question mainstream dominant representation of Arabs pretty early on. I always knew that there was a very gross misrepresentation of Arabs in Hollywood. That was one of the first places I saw it. I also knew the news was misrepresenting us." Schools ranked among the most restrictive spaces, with 85.5% of survey respondents reporting that mostly or only dominant perspectives are presented in K–12 classrooms and textbooks. Thirty-eight percent of respondents reported that only dominant perspectives are presented in K–12 classrooms and textbooks, and another 47.4% indicated that mostly dominant perspectives are presented. Universities fared better than schools, but still 54.0% of survey respondents reported that mostly or only dominant perspectives are presented. Sixty-nine percent of survey respondents reported that some alternative and multiple perspectives are presented through university student clubs, compared to only 46.0% in university classrooms and textbooks.

Finally, the news media are perceived to be the third narrowest space. Thirty percent of respondents believe that the news media only present dominant perspectives, and 52.3% find mostly dominant perspectives are presented. Only 2.2% of respondents reported that multiple perspectives are presented in the news media.

A TROUBLING MISEDUCATION

The survey respondents' top concerns included the Palestine struggle and the war on Iraq; however, 16 of the 18 most pressing concerns[7] related

to domestic issues faced by Arab Americans. The domestic issues are categorized as sources of miseducation, threats to civil liberties, and Arab
American community issues. For the purposes of this chapter, the focus will
be on this troubling miseducation. In response to the open-ended question, almost a quarter of respondents identified racism, discrimination,
and prejudice as the greatest concerns facing Arabs in America. Participants noted pervasive misinformation about Arabs as the reason for such
great misunderstanding and ignorance about Arabs among the general
American population. Bias in the media was identified by respondents as
the third most pressing concern, and 89.4% were concerned about misinformation about Arabs in educational materials. A respondent commented,
"Years after leaving high school, I noticed a young student was reading the
same history text I had in public school in the ninth grade. Re-reading the
section on the Middle East, I was shocked by the bias and misinformation
included in it." Eighty-seven percent of respondents were concerned with
negative stereotypes. A respondent lamented the fact that "My family often
lied about their identity in public to avoid dealing with people's stereotypes. I felt neither safe nor valued in U.S. society."

Seven of the 18 most pressing issues that were identified by the Arab
American respondents had to do with sources of miseducation about Arabs.
These issues are bias in the news media, misinformation about Arabs in
educational materials (e.g., stereotypes in textbooks), Islamophobia, stereotypes, threats to academic freedom, biased teachers/ principals, biased
professors, and the absence of Arabs in educational materials (e.g., textbooks). An American "ideology of miseducation" (Kincheloe & Steinberg,
2006, p. 33) has led to pervasive misunderstandings about Arabs and Islam
among the general public.

An examination of the sources of miseducation is informed by the
four intersecting categories that make up the "societal curriculum"
(Cortes, 2000, p. 18). The categories include the immediate curriculum,
institutional curriculum, serendipitous curriculum, and media curriculum.
The immediate and serendipitous curricula—those learned through
the respondents' lived experiences—do not mesh with much of the
institutional and media curricula that Arab Americans encounter—which
often either do not include Arabs or portray them through stereotypes
and misinformation. Arab American invisibility, orientalism, and negative
stereotypes have contributed to misunderstandings about Arabs (Naber,
2000, 2008; Nieto, 2000; Said, 1978; Shaheen, 2001). Semmerling (2006)
describes the "orientalist fear" that drives the narrow portrayal of Arabs
in film:

> The creation of the "evil" Arabs in American popular film relies on their
> characteristic confrontations with our ideologies and myths, and so the

Arabs, as such a set of Others, are imagined only to exist and act in relation to our ideologies and myths. We have, in a sense, distorted the Arab image with a veneer of our own concerns and self-interests. (p. 29)

The battles over information and representation are also waged in America's universities. Falk (2007) asserts that "academic freedom is today more menaced than at any time since the McCarthy witch hunts and loyalty oaths of the early 1950s" (p. 369). Brand (2007) further notes:

largely as a response to September 11, 2001 attacks, in the last several years, threats to academic freedom have dramatically increased both in number and intensity in the United States ... [and] there is no question that the community of Middle East/North Africa (MENA) scholars has been disproportionately targeted (p. 384)

Federally funded Title VI centers that focus on the Middle East faced increased scrutiny and federal oversight after the 2001 publication of the Washington Institute for Near East Policy's *Ivory Towers on Sand: The Failure of Middle East Studies in America*. MENA scholars were further targeted through the launch of Daniel Pipe's Campus Watch website in 2002 and David Horowitz's 2006 book, *The Professors: The 101 Most Dangerous Academics in America*. According to Brand (2007), "'Campus Watch' began its campaign of intimidation by blacklisting a number of U.S. professors, labeling them terrorist sympathizers because of their writings and statements on Islam, U.S. Middle East policy and Israel"(pp. 390–391). Attempts to narrow discourse and perpetuate the troubling miseducation on such issues appeared to be supported through Daniel Pipes' appointment to the board of the United States Institute for Peace by President George W. Bush in 2003. Falk (2007) describes the threat to academic freedom in the post-9/11 context as an "orchestrated, generously funded multidimensional campaign against genuine democracy in this country that was being waged on many fronts at home while American leaders were circling the globe insisting that other societies become 'democratic'" (p. 369).

ARAB AMERICAN MARGINALIZATION

The post-9/11 context challenged Arab Americans' sense of belonging. Seventy-seven percent of survey respondents reported that they felt a sense of belonging in America prior to 9/11.[8] A shift occurred immediately following 9/11, when 75.2% of respondents indicated that they did *not* feel a sense of belonging, and 57.6% specified that they felt like outsiders. Feelings of alienation grew with the launch of the Iraq War in 2003, with 80.9% of respondents reporting that they did not feel a sense of belonging. Feelings of alienation and marginalization were reported for other key events that followed in the Bush Administration's global war on terrorism, such as the war on Afghanistan and the exposure of the Abu-Ghraib torture and prison abuse scandal. The further marginalization of Arabs in America after 9/11 led respondents to identify a community desire to be accepted and treated as full citizens as a pressing issue facing Arab Americans. As one respondent explained, "The greatest concern is that we are never fully accepted and that we are always treated like we are potential terrorists in the making." Another respondent said this leads to "self-censorship of Arab Americans because they worry about threats to their safety or discrimination." This section discusses the marginalization of Arab Americans by examining the U.S. context through the perceptions and experiences of survey participants, Arab American identity, and how Arab Americans learn about Arabs.

BECOMING PAINFULLY VISIBLE

Arab Americans have been identified as an "invisible minority" (Naber, 2000, 2008; Nieto, 2000). Sixty-five percent of participants who reported that they had felt silenced, invisible, or marginalized for being an Arab American experienced this in school and 54%, in college. A respondent described feeling invisible in school, as "Arab or Arab American culture, history, contributions were absent throughout my educational career in the USA. I felt invisible throughout my primary and secondary schooling." Another participant said that their "ethnicity and culture [were] pretty much ignored and unrecognized [in school]. I was invisible ... and probably because of that, in and out of trouble, and felt that my studies were irrelevant to my perspective."

Sixty-nine percent of respondents who felt they had to stifle part of their identity experienced this in school, and only 30.3% of respondents felt free to express themselves in school. Further, 48.4% of respondents who felt they had to stifle part of their identity experienced this in college. As one participant shared, "It became necessary to hide part of who I am—'Muslim'—to be able to succeed in a mandatory class for my major, taught by a racist Midwest professor.... Never again after that humiliation did I bow down like that."

The political climate has increased the visibility of Arab Americans, but this has been accompanied by increased suspicion and persistently negative images that defined Arabs as the "other." Books (2003) articulated the complexity of such visibility as "feel[ing] like a violent unmasking that reduces and distorts one's humanity" (p. xvi). Survey participants described feeling increasingly marginalized after 9/11, citing experiences with discrimination that resulted from domestic national security policies, such as the Patriot Act. Domestic policies associated with America's war on terrorism that infringe on the civil liberties of all Americans were identified as a major concern by survey participants, with racial profiling ranking as the second most pressing concern (96.9%). Additional areas of concern include detention and political prisoners (88.5 %), denial of due process (88.2%), the use of secret evidence (84.3%), and hate crimes. Some respondents described the hardship they and their families endured. For example, a participant said,

> As I grew older, I began to experience greater hardships with the arrest of my uncle shortly after my twelfth birthday, followed by my father's when I was 17. Both of them were targeted maliciously by a media campaign, in addition to unjust government policies such as secret evidence and the USA Patriot Act.

Believing that a real change was on the way, President Barack Obama's victory on election night of November 4, 2008, was the occasion the respondents reported feeling the greatest sense of belonging as Arab Americans. A participant commented on the fact that "I have felt like an outsider in the U.S. until Obama was elected. I have since had a different experience." Feelings of belonging decreased after Obama's election, which may be attributed to the lack of any significant change on the critical issues that were identified by survey participants.

THE HOME/SCHOOL DIVIDE: ARAB AMERICAN IDENTITY AS A DISCOVERY OF DIFFERENCE

The survey participants were asked to share a personal story of growing up Arab American. More than 50 respondents shared stories where they felt different, where they did not fit in, or that they were out of place. Many participants shared experiences where they felt marginalized, and several used humor to tell their stories. Respondents described the experience of teachers and classmates having difficulty pronouncing their names. A participant recalled,

> Early in my childhood, I remember attending school and the teacher struggling to pronounce my name correctly on the first day. This simple act was the beginning of my sense that I was different somehow from my classmates (and it only grew over time as I matured and learned more about my Palestinian heritage).

Seeking to fit in, several respondents described feeling ashamed of their names when they were young. They temporarily adopted Americanized names to avoid the visibility of their difference, as described by a respondent next:

> Looking back at all the public schools I went to, I noticed that there was no effort to celebrate diversity.... I always had an identity problem. My first name is Hesham and that was difficult for Westerners to say. After a few years of dealing with that, I decided to go by the nickname, Sam. I used to deny that I was Arab until late middle school because of the stereotypes. Looking back, it seems to me that most of the youth were afraid of their cultural stereotypes. Everyone was too worried about fitting in. If the schools promoted cultural diversity, then we could look past exaggerated stereotypes.

Similar experiences were described by respondents who felt the need to stifle part of their identity in college. A respondent explained,

> Although I had always used my full and real name up until high school graduation, for some reason, I introduced myself as "Tim" instead of "Hatem" when I first reached [university]; and everyone continued to call me "Tim" until I was a junior, when I asked people to use my real name.

Some of the respondents recalled feeling embarrassed by their parents, who more loudly represented the difference between their home and school cultures. For example, one participant said students "would often ask me why my mom wore a 'towel' or 'rag' on [her] head, so I would become very embarrassed when my mom would visit the classroom." The lunchroom was described as a space where Arab American difference was spotlighted, as their classmates did not recognize the lunch food they brought from home. A respondent explained, "When I was a kid, I didn't think of myself as Arab American, just an Arab in America. So my lunches were different because I was different and probably didn't belong." Participants described standing out in the lunchroom because of their Muslim dietary restrictions and fasting during Ramadan. For example, "Friends thought it was funny that I didn't eat pork in the elementary school cafeteria. That was probably the first instance of knowing I was different than my peers."

A respondent described the pain of being stereotyped as a child:

> Arriving in the U.S. in the mid-1980s and being labeled "terrorist"—that word had come into popular use at that time. It is hard at age 10 to possess the strength to acknowledge and appreciate your own difference. I think it took many years to overcome those feelings. I could go on forever here.

Some respondents sought assimilation to avoid the difficulties associated with growing up Arab American. For one participant,

My teen years, starting at age 13 until graduating high school, coincided with Desert Storm/first invasion of Iraq. Being Arab and a teenager were very difficult during these years. At times I had to hide my Arab heritage by focusing on my "American" aspect, just to fit in.

Twenty respondents shared stories of being the only Arab or one of very few Arabs in their school or neighborhood as they were growing up. A participant described the experience in these terms:

I remember feeling different and strange compared to my peers, and wanted desperately to fit in. I wished I didn't have dark features, that I was more "White" looking. It was not until after I graduated [from] college in 2003 when I began to find Arab Americans who were able to express themselves and give a voice to my identity. I really began to feel that I belonged to a community, and that there were others that went through the same experience as myself growing up.

Several respondents shared stories of identity development as they found and interacted with a community of Arab Americans. One of them said, "I established an Arab identity at home, an American identity at school, and merged the two when with other Arab Americans." Another participant said, "In high school, I felt foreign, ambiguous, secluded, I had to fit in. When I hung out with people of the same culture it eased the feelings a great deal."

Harassment and Discrimination in American Schools and Universities

Arab Americans faced prejudice in varying forms prior to September 11, 2001 (9/11); however, the discrimination that they experienced grew in frequency and intensity with the post-9/11 backlash (Kimmel & Stout, 2006). Discrimination in the aftermath of 9/11 impacted all aspects of their lives, including employment, education, housing, and religious worship (American-Arab Anti-Discrimination Committee, 2003). Arabs, Muslims, and South Asians in the United States of America have experienced discrimination, hate crimes, and domestic policies that resulted in racial profiling and infringement of civil liberties (American-Arab Anti-Discrimination Committee, 2003). The stress contributed to increased depression and anxiety among the Arab American population, as compared to the general American population (Amer, 2005).

Sixty percent of survey participants who have experienced discrimination indicated that they have faced discrimination in American schools and universities.[9] Compared to earlier schooling experiences where respondents reported that they were "never encouraged to express [their] culture ... and kids would make fun of anyone who was different," the high school experience seemed to have somewhat improved. As a respondent reflected, "The younger years I did not feel positively and knowledgeable about being Arab American, but in high school that changed and I was embraced in my educational environment." Another participant described being "more open with my friends [in high school] as far as talking about myself as an Arab American and sharing Arab culture."

While discrimination seems to manifest itself equally in school and university settings, universities more effectively provide students with opportunities to express themselves. The respondents were asked to indicate if they had the opportunity to share their history or express their culture in these educational contexts and other sites of learning. The pattern holds that schools are a more restrictive space than universities for such expression, with only 27.9% of survey participants indicating that they have had an opportunity to share their history in school and 41.4% reporting an opportunity to express their culture. The university setting provided an opportunity for 52.5% of survey participants to share their history and 60.1% to express their culture.

Participants shared experiences of harassment and discrimination, many of which came during the Gulf War and after 9/11. Several respondents described name-calling that escalated with the rise in U.S.–Arab tensions. They shared stories of being threatened, bullied, and told to "go home." Some reported that they were "called names, spit on, and physically attacked" or "called a sand nigger, A-rab, raghead, and terrorist because I am outspoken about being Arab and the school did nothing to help me." A respondent described feeling "very unsafe after 9/11 and was harassed by people [in high school] because of my hijab [headscarf]. I hated having to explain myself all of the time." That respondent felt "lucky to have a strong MSA [Muslim Student Association]" at school.

Several participants shared experiences where they felt intimidated by physical threats by other students at school. During the Gulf War, a high school student was

> threatened in the girl's bathroom by a boy who held a knife to my throat and said, "Get out of town you fucking Arab piece of shit! You don't belong in America bitch." I was very afraid to go to school after that experience. My family decided to sell their business and move again for my safety.

Another respondent said:

> For the most part, being Arab American isn't a hard thing to do. However, right around the time of September 11, 2001, it was kind of hard, simply for the fact that I am a Muslim woman who wears the headscarf. I did attend a

diverse high school; however, during that period of time, fear was definitely heightened amongst my peers. I did experience a few personal verbal and physical threats, mainly by young males, but it didn't seem to bother me too much (as they were just threats, nothing really happened). Another incident to point out, the local masjid [mosque] that I sometimes attended had a drive-by shooting, resulting in no casualties. These two incidents may have been a little hard at the time, but every day my faith kept me going.

One of the participants described the vandalism of his home during the same time period:

I was walking home from school. I was in the 6th grade. I remember it being snowy.... I was reaching our home on my walk home and this was during the First Gulf War. As I reached our garage door, the words "Go back home you animal" were spray painted on the door of the garage. I stared at it for like ten minutes, letting the snow melt on my Arab skin. That's when I knew I was different.

Early Encounters With Miseducation

Participants described difficult encounters with educators, where they felt a burden of representing perspectives that were contrary to their teachers' viewpoint, yet they did not feel equipped with the necessary knowledge. One of the respondents recalled a "physics teacher in high school [saying] that Arabs never contributed anything to civilization.... I argued with him but had no facts to back me up. I remember feeling angry about that." A survey participant described a similar frustration of

feeling forced to become a spokesperson on Middle East issues, from the Gulf War to Islam to the Persian Gulf War to 9/11, to explain and defend Arab values and culture to people who really don't seem to want to hear the full context and just want a bullet-point answer. The worst part is that in most cases, I simply do not know enough to educate others on many of these topics but I feel that saying something is better than nothing.

Respondents also shared stories of their discomfort with some of their assignments in school. For example, one of the artists recalled a fifth grade assignment:

to write a letter to George Bush Sr. expressing how we supported his war on Iraq, Desert Storm. We each had fancy paper and pen and [they were] going to be mailed together. I remember I wrote a bunch of nothing, scribbled and drenched my paper in white-out. It was a very uncomfortable experience for me as a child.

Palestinian American respondents described experiences where teachers denied their Palestinian identity because Palestine was not represented as a country on modern maps. A respondent described "culture day" in elementary school—"I was the last kid in the class sitting next to the globe looking for the map of 'Palestine' and couldn't find it ... everyone else had found their countries, and I kinda felt like I wanted to be from Italy, 'cause it was so convenient and normal."

According to Abu El-Haj (2006), "Educators need a new framework for understanding the particular equity issues that Muslim Arab youth face in U.S. schools," adding that "focusing on understanding culture is an important but insufficient framework for addressing [their] needs" (p. 15). Instead, Abu El-Haj asserts that educators must "attend to the particular processes of racial subordination to which these youth are subjected within and outside of schools" (p. 15). The survey respondents further support that such processes are at play in American schools, even in early elementary school.

Arab Americans Learning About Themselves

Learning to negotiate the cultural landscape was a task that some respondents felt they were left to navigate on their own. One respondent explained:

> I learned about my family's story and gradually developed my political understanding of Palestine, as well as the Arab American experience, through intensive self-study and exploration. Many Palestinian and other Arab Americans I know have been in a similar boat, where they have had to self-educate, in the absence of effective cultural and political institutions that would facilitate this process.

Survey participants were asked to share their experiences learning about Arabs and Arab Americans across multiple sites of education. While 88.2% of participants reported that they had read at least one book by an Arab author, only 22.4% reported that they had read it in school, and 62.0% read it in college. Only 17.4% of survey participants reported that they had learned about Arab history in school, compared to 43.3% who studied Arab history in college. Twenty-two percent of respondents learned about Arab contributions to civilization in school, and 36.5% learned about them in college. Only 6.5% of respondents learned about Arab American contributions to American society in school, and 23.6% learned about them in college. The survey respondents most often learned about Arab history (62.2%) and contributions to civilization (59.0%) at home.

More participants reported that they learned about the history and contributions of Arabs and Arab Americans at university than in school. This is likely due to the broader selection of courses that are offered at the university and the opportunity for students to select their majors, courses, and professors. Nineteen percent of respondents reported that they were instructed by at least one Arab teacher at school, and 56.9% took a course with at least one Arab professor in college. Eighty-eight percent of respondents reported reading the work of at least one Arab author. Twenty-two percent of respondents reported reading an Arab author's work in school, and 62.0% read them in college. When provided the opportunity, Arab American students seek out courses and professors to learn about Arab history and culture. A participant rejoiced at having had "great Arab American professors who really helped me a great deal."

Universities have provided greater academic freedom than schools, including greater freedom of expression and opportunities for multiple perspectives to be shared. Consistent with this finding, more survey participants felt a sense of belonging in universities (77.7%) than schools (56.6%). The greater sense of belonging at university is supported by participants' exposure to and participation in student clubs, which many participants noted had impacted their Arab American identity.

Respondents described an evolution of ethnic pride over time, alongside the formation of their Arab American identity. While 90.6% of respondents reported that they felt proud to be Arab American, only 34.1% reported that they felt proud to be Arab American in school. This compares to 64% percent who felt proud to be Arab American when they were in college. Many respondents commented on the influence of their friends and student organizing experiences on the development of their Arab American identity: "I enjoyed college much more than high school." In another participant's view, "I don't remember how my Arab American identity crystallized, but I know that it happened through university-based organizing." A third participant is happy for making the right decision: "Definitely joining the Arab Club at school, that was my greatest influence.... They helped me be proud of being Arab."

The late Palestinian American scholar and public intellectual, Edward Said (1935–2003), has had a significant impact on the identity of Arab Americans. Said's (1978) seminal, work, *Orientalism*, contributed to the foundation of postcolonial studies. More than any other individual, respondents cited Edward Said as having the greatest influence on their Arab American identity. Several participants saw in Said the one who inspired them to engage in the path of critical inquiry. A respondent proffered:

> One of my greatest influences is Professor Edward Said, and for quite simple reasons—he was Palestinian, and was a respected scholar, professor, thinker,

writer, musician, and cross-cultural peace activist. He embodied everything positive about Palestinian culture, and the artistic/philosophical potential of every Palestinian/Arab American. His existence proved that we can translate negative aspects of the Palestinian experience into something truly enlightening, emboldening, and constructive.

A participant noted that Edward Said was "the first scholar I was introduced to who spoke about the question of identity and inspired me to research, think, observe, and feel in a deeper, more insightful way." Another respondent found he "gave my Arab American identity a moral, political, culturally rich, and critical dimension."

Negotiating Us Versus Them

More than 60% of survey respondents reported that their primary identity is a hybrid between their Arab heritage and American—a hybrid of "us" and "them." One-third of respondents, however, did not identify as American. One participant bemoans a lack of sense of belonging to the U.S. as a nation: "I do not feel a sense of belonging in the USA." For another respondent who described the influence of the political climate in the U.S. on their identity formation, "By creating and fueling 'us' vs. 'them' hatred, he [President George W. Bush] made me only cling to the Arab and Muslim part of my identity even more."

Given the sociopolitical climate and human need to belong, several survey participants felt moved to choose one identity or the other—either Arab or American. A participant noted that, "Following [the] 9/11 attacks, I was not feeling comfortable expressing my identity as an Arab/Muslim American." Another respondent added, "The first time I felt being Arab was on 9/11. Before then it was in the background; after 9/11, it came to the forefront."

The experience of being "othered" led many Arab American respondents to identify with and take pride in their difference. Several respondents described their experience in terms of the fabricated binary of "us" vs. "them"— "American" vs. "Arab," "American" vs. "Muslim." For one of the participants, "I always knew I was Arab; more specifically I always knew I was Palestinian from the village of Ramoun. Not being Americanized was essentially like a moral litmus test in my family." Some of the participants described their identification with a Muslim identity in relation to feeling different; for example, "Being Muslim probably made me more different than being Arab—Ramadan, praying five times [a day], etc." Another respondent said, "Loneliness, feeling of being an outcast and a stranger all my life made my PRIDE in my identity (Islam) much stronger."

Several respondents described the impact of 9/11 on their identity. A participant who was in class the morning of 9/11 became defensive of the Arab community: "Definite wake up call to my own identity." Another respondent opined:

> I will never forget the moment I owned my "Arab-ness." As corny and cliché as it sounds, it literally happened the day of September 11th. That day, when I came home from a class at college my father instructed me and my older brother to follow a new set of rules to avoid any potential threat on our life. One was to come home at 7:00 p.m. and another was to live below the radar. I quickly countered what I believed to be absurd demands on our personal freedom by reassuring my father, "Dad, don't even worry, most of these people think I'm Mexican anyway." And sotto voce, I muttered, "Thank God I look Mexican." And less than a split second my whole personal and worldview changed—that's when I affirmed my Arabness and proclaimed "Thank God? What? I'm Arab and I don't care what people think."

A respondent described the university experience during 9/11 as "the time in my life when I felt the most Arab American and the most marginalized." One of the participants described a university class discussion after 9/11. "People were very emotional and accusative. Being told to my face that internment for all Arabs was the only logical option to keep the country safe. Being accused of carrying a bomb at restaurants." A survey participant who reported the realization of being Arab American after the 9/11 attacks said, "I never felt different from my college freshmen peers, but that attack changed everything. The attack completely altered my existence; it gave me a purpose. It made me realize how underrepresented my community is, and how in danger we were because of that."

In his 1999 autobiography, *Out of Place*, Said discusses the experience of having one foot in each culture, Arab and American. Several respondents shared similar experiences of always feeling out of place. This "balancing act between the two cultures" was described by several respondents, with one participant noting that "I have never really felt complete belonging anywhere." A survey participant described the journey out of identity confusion, saying:

> I used to think that being both Arab and American, having a foot in both worlds, was confusing and alienating, that I really didn't belong squarely in either one. But over the years I have realized that it is a gift to have the experience of two cultures, two languages, and that it enriches me as a person.

Edward Said (1999) said: "With so many dissonances in my life I have learned actually to prefer being not quite right and out of place" (p. 295). Advocating for "coexistence with the preservation of difference" (2003),

Said exemplified what it means to be "authentically rooted in more than one place" (1998).

Consistent with Said's notion of multiple roots, several participants addressed the influence of their parents in developing a balanced identity that includes the best of both cultures and allows for the coexistence of their Arab and American identities. A participant noted that his parents "shared with me the beauty of our culture and heritage and taught me to be very proud of my identity." Another respondent recalled, "My parents constantly emphasized both our Arab identity and our American identity, and would not apologize for either." The father of one participant had "taught me to hold onto my values while exercising my rights as an American." Emphasizing the common humanity of all cultures, a respondent described how parents:

> inspire me to embrace all the cultures that I am a part of—particularly the parts that resonate with my ideals—and also to embrace other cultures that I learn about through friendships and experience. As a result, I increasingly see myself as a human being more so than as any other label.

CONCLUDING NOTES: MOVING DEMOCRACY FORWARD BY BROADENING PUBLIC DISCOURSE AND RECENTERING FREEDOM AND PLURALISM

Arab Americans have a significant role to play in moving the democratic project forward in America by recentering freedom and pluralism. Their collective experience has provided the opportunity for them to take responsibility for educating themselves, broadening public discourse and countering miseducation by articulating their narratives, sharing alternate perspectives, and educating other Americans through and contributing to the democratic project that is always in the making by taking action on pressing issues. Participants reported working on a wide range of social justice issues—beyond the issues that impact Arabs and Arab Americans— and a number of them described their work on within a broader framework of human rights and civil liberties. As one participant reflected:

> The issues facing Arabs are human made as are all oppressive issues; however, they have been institutionalized and made to be a systemic construct. If we work on ourselves to understand the frameworks and discourses, then we start to battle the issues by addressing the root problems, which inform these structures, we can succeed in changing them.

Henry Giroux (2005) contends that

Educators and other cultural workers [must] struggle to preserve and revital-
ize those institutional spaces, forums, and public spheres that support and
defend critical education, help students come to terms with their own power
as individuals and social agents, and reclaim those non-market values such
as caring, community, trust, conviction, and courage that are vital to a sub-
stantive democracy.

Exemplifying the relationship between conscientization and praxis,
most survey participants reported that they first became active through
their formal studies in college/graduate school and through informal education in student clubs. As one respondent said,

In college I was introduced to postcolonial literature that intrigued me to
learn more about my history as an Arab and this combined with my emotional sentiment towards the political turmoil in the Arab world made me
more active and able to create and organize innovative projects and events.

Arab American communities and organizations provided a context for
many respondents to get involved. According to Cainkar (2009),

The post-9/11 experience for Arab and Muslim Americans reveals a para-
doxical historical moment. At the same time as members of these groups
have since 9/11 experienced extensive institutional discrimination, government targeting (mainly focused on men), and public attacks (largely focused
on women and Islamic religious institutions), they have also experienced
enhanced civic inclusion. Arab Americans and Muslim Americans, their organizations and institutions, have become visible players in the American
public square to a greater degree than at any previous time in American history—with the significant exception of African American Muslims, who have
a decades-long history of engagement in America society.... This perhaps
unexpected positive outcome of post-9/11 events emerged from the dialectic
that was put into motion when state repression, public attacks, and popular
vilification rather quickly reached a level that was intolerable to Arab and
Muslim Americans, to a sector of American civic institutions, and to many
individuals in the United States. (p. 263)

A few of the respondents reported that their earliest involvement was
school-based. For example, a participant described efforts to end the bullying that Arab Americans were experiencing in their school during the
Gulf War. They

started a group to help protect those that could not protect themselves and
who needed someone to watch out for them.... This gave hope for some to
stand up and be strong and not let discrimination and hatred take over." Another respondent shared an experience countering the local media's misinformation on their Islamic school as a "terrorist breeding ground. My peers

countered these news outlets with letters and interviews, and ... tried to make
our charitable activities more visible to the wider community.

Some survey participants indicated that their travels to Arab countries
and personal experiences with discrimination moved them to get involved.
Many respondents spoke of key events that activated them, such as the
Palestinian intifada (uprising) of the 1980s, the Israeli invasion of Lebanon
in 1982, the Sabra and Shatila massacres, the 1985 assassination of Arab
American Alex Odeh in California, the Gulf War, the start of the Al-Aqsa
intifada in September 2000, and 9/11. A participant noted, "After 9/11, I
realized that most Americans, as the rest of the world, don't know much
about Arab Americans and Arabs in general."

The survey asked participants to share the factors that contributed to
their growth and empowerment as activists. Their responses included
intrinsic motivators, such as a sense of public service, as well as extrin-
sic factors like mentors and "family and friends encouraging me to get
involved." The most common response was connections with communities, including non-Arab communities. A respondent attributed personal
growth and empowerment to "a strong and creative community that is
always inspiring me to grow and engage."

The second most common factor that contributed to respondents'
growth and empowerment was one's own awareness and education. For
one respondent, "The broadening of my intellectual and spiritual capacity
made me more compelled to become an activist." Participants acknowledge
the important role of education and self-reflection in their growth. They
further addressed the evolution of their confidence and empowerment as
they continued to learn, gained knowledge and experience, and sharp-
ened their skills (e.g., researching, writing, speaking). Some respondents
noted the influence of professors and mentors who served as role models
for them. Others spoke of "taking my own education into my own hands."
This respondent elaborated as follows:

> I didn't learn much about my own history in college so I created an
> independent study where I researched Arab feminism. I began to learn about
> the struggles of Arab women and became more empowered by studying how
> they resisted. In particular, I found deep connections with Arab women poets.

Finally, participants shared intrinsic factors that contributed to their
growth and empowerment as activists, including a sense of justice, moral
responsibility, identity and ethnic pride, and faith-based values. A respondent explained being driven by "the simple belief that one must stand up
and be counted. It is my moral responsibility to understand the struggles
and hardships my family must live with on a daily basis, and it is my duty

to support any efforts made to improve the conditions in which they live."
Similarly, another participant vented his feelings:

> I have always felt the need to stand up for what's right, fair, and just. So I
> have always been vocal, even since I was in junior high, trying to explain to
> my classmates what Palestine is and why there isn't a country named Pales-
> tine on the map, etc. As the years grew and especially once I got to college,
> more opportunities became available to become involved in activism and
> organizing. And so I did.

REFERENCES

Abu El-Haj, T. R. (2006). Race, politics, and Arab American youth: Shifting frame-works for conceptualizing educational equity. *Educational Policy, 20*(1), 13-34.

Amer, M. (2005). *Arab American mental health in the post September 11 era: Acculturation, stress, and coping.* Unpublished Dissertation, University of Toledo, Toledo, OH.

American-Arab Anti-Discrimination Committee (ADC). (2003). *Report on hate crimes & discrimination against Arab Americans: The post-September 11 backlash— September 11, 2001 to October 11, 2002.* Washington, DC: International Graphics.

Books, S. (Ed.). (2003). *Invisible children in the society and its schools* (2nd ed.). Mahwah, NJ: Lawrence Erlbaum Associates.

Brand, L. A. (2007). Middle East studies and academic freedom: Challenges at home and abroad. *International Studies Perspectives, 8*(4), 384–395.

Brittingham, A., & de la Cruz, G. P. (2005). *We the people of Arab ancestry in the United States: Census 2000 Special Reports.* Washington, DC: U.S. Department of Commerce, Economics and Statistics Administration, U.S. Census Bureau.

Cainkar, L. A. (2009). *Homeland insecurity: The Arab American and Muslim American experience after 9/11.* New York, NY: Russell Sage Foundation.

Cortes, C. E. (2000). *The children are watching: How the media teach about diversity.* New York, NY: Teachers College Press.

de la Cruz, G. P., & Brittingham, A. (2003). *The Arab population: 2000.* Census 2000 Brief. Washington, DC: U.S. Department of Commerce, Economics and Statistics Administration, U.S. Census Bureau.

Dewey, J. (1916). *Democracy and education.* New York, NY: The MacMillan Company.

Falk, R. (2007). Academic freedom under siege. *International Studies Perspectives, 8*(4), 369–375.

Gates, H. L., Jr. (1992). "Ethnic and minority" studies. Retrieved from http://web.nwe.ufl.edu/~stripp/2504/gates1.pdf

Giroux, H. (2005, January 2). Cultural studies in dark times: Public pedagogy and the challenge of neoliberalism. *Fast Capitalism.* Retrieved from http://www.henryagiroux.com/online_articles/DarkTimes.htm

Giroux, H. (2006). Radical pedagogy and the terror of neoliberalism: Rethinking the significance of cultural politics. In A. Dirlik (Ed.), *Pedagogies of the global: Knowledge in the human interest.* Boulder, CO: Paradigm.

Greene, M. (1995). *Releasing the imagination: Essays on education, the arts, and social change.* San Francisco, CA: Jossey-Bass.

Hochschild, J., & Burch, T. (2007). Contingent public policies and the stability of racial hierarchy: Lessons from immigration and census policy. In I. Shapiro & S. Bedi (Eds.), *Political contingency: Studying the unexpected, the accidental, and the unforeseen.* New York, NY: New York University Press.

Horowitz, D. (2006). *The professors: The 101 most dangerous academics in America.* Washington, DC: Regnery.

Kimmel, P. R., & Stout, C. E. (Eds.). (2006). *Collateral damage: The psychological consequences of America's war on terrorism.* Westport, CT: Praeger.

Kincheloe, J. L., & Steinberg, S. R. (2006). An ideology of miseducation: Countering the pedagogy of empire. *Cultural Studies Critical Methodologies, 6*(1), 33–51.

Kramer, M. (2001). *Ivory Towers on Sand: The failure of Middle Eastern studies in America.* Washington, DC: Washington Institute for Near East Policy.

Naber, N. (2000). Ambiguous insiders: An investigation of Arab American invisibility. *Ethnic and Racial Studies, 23*(1), 37–61.

Naber, N. (2008). Introduction: Arab Americans and U.S. racial formations. In A. Jamal & N. Naber (Eds.), *Race and Arab Americans before and after 9/11: From invisible citizens to visible subjects.* Syracuse, NY: Syracuse University Press.

Nieto, S. (2000). *Affirming diversity: The sociopolitical context of multicultural education* (3rd ed.). New York, NY: Longman.

Rury, J. L. (2005). *Education and social change: Themes in the history of American schooling* (2nd ed.). Mahwah, NJ: Lawrence Erlbaum Associates.

Said, E. W. (1978). *Orientalism.* New York, NY: Random House.

Said, E. W. (1998). *The myth of the "clash of civilizations."* University of Massachusetts, Amherst. Retrieved from http://www.mediaed.org/cgi-bin/commerce.cgi?preadd=action&key=404

Said, E. W. (1999). *Out of place: A memoir.* New York, NY: Alfred A. Knopf.

Said, E. W. (2003). The clash of definitions. In L. M. Alcoff & E. Mendieta (Eds.), *Identities: Race, class, gender, and nationality* (pp. 333–335). Malden, MA: Blackwell.

Semmerling, T. J. (2006). *"Evil" Arabs in American popular film.* Austin, TX: University of Texas Press.

Shaheen, J. (2001). *Reel bad Arabs: How Hollywood vilifies a people.* Brooklyn, NY: Olive Branch Press.

Suleiman, M. W. (Ed.). (1999). *Arabs in America: Building a new future.* Philadelphia, PA: Temple University.

West, C. (2004). *Democracy matters: Winning the fight against imperialism.* New York, NY: Penguin Press.

CHAPTER 6

BEST APPROACHES TO LITERACY INSTRUCTION TO ENGLISH LANGUAGE LEARNERS

Cultural Conflicts and Compromises

Guofang Li

Growing immigration in North America is causing many mainstream teachers to become English as a second language (ESL) teachers by default. Increasingly, they struggle with not only effective pedagogical approaches of helping students acquire a new language while mastering academic content, but also with challenges of dealing with different cultural under-standings, assumptions, and expectations about their instructional practices from parents who are of culturally and linguistically different backgrounds. Such different cultural understandings, assumptions, and expectations, if not addressed, often result in school–home mismatch and become a risk factor for immigrant and minority students' learning (Au, 1998; Golden-berg & Gallimore, 1995; Heath, 1983; Ogbu, 1982; Valdés, 1996).

There is a proliferation of studies on what constitutes best instructional approaches in literacy instruction for mainstream students (Gambrell & Mazzoni, 1999; Morrow & Gambrell, 2011; Wharton-McDonald, Pressley,

& Hampston, 1998). However, few studies have focused on what constitutes best approaches of second language and literacy instruction for language minority students. Much research that has explored literacy instruction for linguistically diverse students often reflects only teacher and researcher perspectives and do not address the role of minority culture in literacy pedagogy. No studies thus far have included the perspectives of various stakeholders such as minority parents in the discussion of how literacy should be taught.

Historically, minority parents from diverse cultural backgrounds are often considered to be at a "deficit" and incapable of providing valuable contributions to their children's education (Goldenberg, 1987; Harry, 1992; Moll & Diaz, 1993). However, studies on minority parents' involvement in their children's education at home have suggested that minority parents, despite their socioeconomic status, are capable of helping their children and providing valuable insight into their children's learning, in and out of school (Goldenberg, 1987; Lazar & Weisberg, 1996; Li, 2004). In fact, research has demonstrated that the failure of schools to include parents' voice and address their ideas and perspectives about schooling often creates barriers for students' learning and achievement (Corson, 1992; Harry, 1992; Li, 2003, 2004).

This chapter extends current research by exploring effective literacy instruction from Asian parents' perspectives. In particular, the focus of the discussion is on the cultural accords and discords between mainstream teachers and Chinese immigrant parents about the nature of literacy instruction and schooling.

CULTURAL MODELS OF LITERACY PEDAGOGY

From a socioconstructivist perspective, literacy learning is seen as a dynamic process that involves complex social relationships that the learners form with members of their particular sociocultural contexts, such as the mainstream teachers and the Chinese parents in this discussion. Each of these members represents a voice of learning and knowing and, thus, forms a "dialogized heteroglossia," or multivoicedness, in which multiple layers of cultural values are embodied (Bakhtin, 1981, p. 272). According to Gee (1989), the dialogized heteroglossia can be categorized into two overarching domains: the primary Discourse of the home and community, and the secondary Discourses, such as the public schools. Nested in these two sociocultural domains are different literacy belief systems that define distinct identities within the different discourses (Bakhtin, 1981).

From a sociocultural perspective, literacy is part of culture (Schieffelin, 1986; Street, 1993). People of a given culture practice literacy in ways that reflect what they value and what they do; beliefs of what literacy is and what it means vary from culture to culture. Thus, shaped by different social and cultural norms, literacy practices—their functions, meanings, and methods of transmission and instruction—vary from one cultural group to another (Langer, 1987). In cross-cultural contexts, the meanings of literacy practices arise in ongoing interactions and negotiations between individuals or groups from different cultural backgrounds (Spradley & McCurdy, 2011). In this sense, literacy practices in cross-cultural contexts are processes through which different cultural voices and understandings come into contact (Wertsch, 1991). In this discussion, mainstream teachers' literacy instruction in school and minority parents' involvement at home are seen as practices that are related to their respective cultural beliefs as well as the ongoing negotiations and interactions between the two groups.

The different cultural beliefs between mainstream teachers and minority parents are different cultural models that represent their understandings of how the world works shared within their respective communities and groups (D'Andrade & Strauss, 1992; Holland & Quinn, 1987). According to Gee (1996, 1999), a cultural model not only defines what is normal and to be expected, but also sets up what counts as non-normal and threatening in certain contexts. Therefore, cultural models often involve certain viewpoints about what is right and wrong and what can or cannot be done to solve problems in the world. As Gee points out, such functions often result in rendering exclusionary actions and creating and upholding stereotypes (Gee, 1996).

Research has demonstrated that the dynamics and processes of different cultural models of literacy practices can have a significant impact on minority achievement and school reform (Gallimore & Goldenberg, 2001). Since cultural models carry within them values and perspectives on people and reality, different cultural models can "conflict in their content, in how they are used, and in values and perspectives they carry" (Gee, 1996, p. 90). For minority students who come from diverse backgrounds, the cultural models of their own home cultures can conflict seriously with those of the mainstream culture (Gee, 1996).

Studies on immigrant and minority groups' literacy practices suggest that immigrant parents differ significantly in their cultural models of learning and their educational values, beliefs, and actions from their mainstream counterparts (e.g., Goldenberg & Gallimore, 1995; Heath, 1983; Li, 2002; Valdés, 1996). Taking literacy instruction, for example, several researchers who focus on different cultural groups (e.g., African Americans and Latinos) have suggested that there exists cultural conflict between minority and mainstream beliefs on effective practices. While the mainstream cultural models of literacy instruction emphasize meaning-based instruction such as a meaning-based approach (top-down), many immigrant and minority parents prefer more of a phonics approach (bottom-up, skill-based) to begin literacy instruction. Delpit (1988, 1995) and Willis (1995), in their seminal work on cultural conflicts in mainstream classrooms, suggest that African American teachers and parents may not share mainstream beliefs about a whole-language approach to literacy instruction and may prefer more skill-based approaches. Similarly, Gallimore and Goldenberg (2001) and Reyes (1992) demonstrated that Latino parents also favored a bottom-up, skill-based cultural model of literacy instruction over a whole-language approach that is commonly practiced in the U.S. classrooms. Gunderson (2001) explains that the mainstream cultural models (e.g., the whole-language approaches) are built on the "natural" language acquisition of middle-class European American children, and they may be in opposition to beliefs held by parents and students from different cultural traditions. Thus, without attending to the different cultural models of literacy instruction, implementing a "one-size-fits-all" (p. 265) mainstream cultural model may put some minority children at a disadvantage while giving an advantage to mainstream children (Reyes, 1992; Willis, 1995).

ASIAN PARENTS AND MAINSTREAM SCHOOLS: THE CHINESE PERSPECTIVES

Previous studies on Chinese immigrants in North America have concluded that Chinese immigrant parents placed paramount importance on education, and their high expectations for their children's education are reported to have determining effects on their children's academic performance (Li, 2002; Peng & Wright, 1994; Siu, 1994; Zhang & Carrasquillo, 1995). In a comparative study, Chao (1996) concludes that in comparison with their European American counterparts, Chinese parents not only place greater value on education and are willing to invest more in their children's education, but also use a more direct intervention approach (e.g., through teaching and tutoring at home) to their children's schooling and learning and convey a much stronger belief that they can play a significant role in their children's school success.

The Chinese parents' cultural models of literacy are different from the mainstream literacy pedagogy (e.g., the whole-language perspectives) adopted in many Canadian and American mainstream classrooms (Anderson & Gunderson, 1997; Li, 2003, 2004). Research has found that Chinese immigrant parents hold different beliefs about specific literacy instruction and practices from mainstream parents (Zhang, Ollila, & Harvey, 1998). In another comparative study of parents' beliefs about reading and writing, Anderson (1995) reports that Chinese parents are more concerned with basic literacy skills and with monitoring and correcting performance such as teaching a child to print and write properly, checking for understanding of what a child has read, teaching a child how to spell correctly, and having a child recite a story she or he has read; they believe these are the most important things they can do to help with their child's literacy learning. Similarly, Anderson and Gunderson (1997) find that Chinese immigrant parents believe that accuracy and precision are important from the beginning and see little value in children's early attempts at reading or invented spelling, and they view language learning as skills accumulation and emphasize rote memorization.

Li (2004, 2006), in her research on middle-class Asian immigrant parents and mainstream Canadian teachers' battles over what counts as the best literacy instructional method, reports that mainstream teachers prefer a whole-language approach to literacy instruction with added components for basic literacy skills such as vocabulary and phonics instruction. Although the Chinese parents liked the practicality and flexibility of the mainstream teachers' approaches, they expressed overriding concerns about lack of discrete skills instruction (i.e., reading and writing strategies, grammar, and vocabulary) and homework (i.e., the nature and the amount of assignments). They opposed the integration of different subject areas and preferred that they be taught separately. Differing from the teachers' monolingual orientation, the parents expected their children to become bilingual and biliterate. When these concerns were not addressed at school, the parents took action outside school (e.g., sending their children to private tutoring classes) to pursue their own beliefs.

Comparative research on Chinese and European American families' beliefs and practices on young children's education (e.g., Chao, 1996; Huntsinger, Jose, Larson, Krieg, & Shaligram, 2000; Stevenson, Lee, & Mu, 2013) has concluded that culture shapes what parents believe and what practices they employ to socialize their children for academic achievement. Chinese immigrant parents are found to prefer more didactic methods for teaching mathematics, vocabulary, and reading, and often use them at home to supplement school learning (Huntsinger et al., 2000; Huntsinger, Jose, Rudden, Luo, & Krieg, 2001; Li, 2002, 2003; Stevenson, Lee & Mu, 2013). The Chinese parents' preferred teaching style is influenced by the cultural models of instruction in their country of origin (Hong Kong and mainland China). Chinese and Hong Kong elementary schooling can be characterized as teacher-centered, academic-oriented, and test-driven (Carron & Châu, 1996; Li, 2006).

In China (and other Asian countries), this teacher-centered, whole-class teaching style is employed in all the core subjects such as Chinese, mathematics, and English, and it is supported by both Chinese teachers and parents. This cultural model is different from the student-centered, communicative nature of meaning-based instruction that is supported by many teachers in Canada. Researchers on English curriculum innovation in Asian settings (e.g., Hong Kong) believe that there exist profound cultural and philosophical differences between the East and the West (Carless, 1998; Morris & Lo, 2000). For example, the East may place more emphasis on "knowledge building" through teacher-centered instruction, while the West may focus more on learners' "process of knowing" (Wells, 1998). As Morris and Lo (2000) summarized, the differences between the two approaches could simply be portrayed as "a clash between an innovation based on Western cultural precepts and a Chinese/Confucian culture" (p. 176).

The cultural clashes, in turn, affect what parents do at home with their children to compromise with mainstream schooling. Research on Chinese immigrants' family literacy practices suggests that Chinese parents enforce their literacy beliefs through active involvement in their children's learning at home (Li, 2002; Xu, 1999). For example, Chinese parents often ask their children to not only repeat reading a story in order to memorize, but also ask them to copy the text several times in order to practice writing at home (Li, 2002; Townsend & Fu, 1998). Li (2002) discovered that middle-class Chinese parents also help their children's English language learning by directly teaching them reading and writing skills including new vocabularies. They use a variety of tools and strategies such as using flash cards, visuals, and their children's knowledge in Chinese to target unknown words.

Another strategy is through after-school tutoring programs. In Li's (2006) study, the middle-class parents were unsatisfied with school literacy instruction and, as a response, and they "educationalize their children's learning at home by sending them to a variety of study activities after school" (p. 207). These activities include math, English, piano lessons, Chinese classes, and sports activities. In fact, some children in the study took the after-school classes more seriously than their regular classes at school. They sometimes do not do the homework assigned by the teachers but treat the homework from tutoring classes much more seriously. Furthermore, the parents also organized political campaigns in the community to establish a traditional school that is more aligned with their own cultural and educational beliefs.

LEARNING FROM THE CHINESE PERSPECTIVES: IMPLICATIONS

These antithetical beliefs between Chinese parents and mainstream teachers suggest that literacy instruction is not simply a pedagogical matter, but also a cultural phenomenon. Mainstream teachers and parents who came from different cultural traditions held different perceptions of not only what literacy is, but also how it should be taught (Anderson, 1995; Gunderson, 1997). These different cultural models of literacy also became a motivational force that informs their respective pedagogical actions in school and at home (Holland & Quinn, 1987; Strauss, 1992). As Li (2006) suggests, the parents' and the teachers' different culturally informed pedagogical practices have significant consequences on the children's learning experiences in school and at home—they suffer not only cultural discontinuity, but also the heavy burden of double workload from both school and home.

To better serve the needs of the linguistically and culturally diverse students, it is important to understand literacy instruction from different cultural points of view, especially those of minority groups. From such a cultural lens, the teacher's meaning-based literacy instruction, as well as the parents' skill-based orientation, can be seen as one of the multiple ways literacy instruction can be used as a complementary resource. The whole-language approach, for example, can be seen as "a pedagogical phenomenon uniquely imbued with mainstream North American cultural features" (Gunderson, 2001, p. 246). It represents Eurocentric values and beliefs that are not necessarily shared by minority groups from different cultural traditions. However, these values and beliefs form the core of the educational thought that guides curriculum development and instructional practices (Corson, 1992). The domination of mainstream cultural models of literacy pedagogy often means the exclusion and marginalization of other minority cultural models in school (Gee, 1996). The Chinese parents' different understandings of literacy instruction suggest that monocultural views of curriculum and instruction must be changed to include minority voices. If we continue to view education from a "mainstream" viewpoint that focuses on European values and beliefs in schools with multicultural population, it will lead to the disempowerment and the disabling of students from dominated backgrounds (Au, 2001; Corson, 1992; Gunderson, 2001; Ladson-Billings, 1995).

Equally, from a cultural point of view, the skill-based approach should not be regarded a simple pedagogical technique that is reductive to learning (Bomer, 1998; Spiegel, 1999; Wells, 1998). Rather, it should be viewed as part of the cultural models of literacy pedagogy in which many minority groups socialize their children into learning. As Gunderson (2001) points out:

> It is not enough simply to dismiss divergent views as wrong. Traditional schooling clearly works for some individuals within the established system— that is, it empowers some students to acquire the knowledge they need to be successful in school and subsequently class-stratified society. (p. 265)

The findings on mainstream teachers' and Chinese parents' views on literacy instruction make two crucial points for literacy education of linguistically and culturally diverse students. First, the different perspectives illustrate that the conceptions of how literacy should be taught are social constructions that are embedded in specific cultural beliefs. Second, the dichotomous positions between the teacher and the parents show that the conflicts between the two parties parallel the ongoing discussion on effective literacy instruction in the field (see Chall, 1996, 2000). Such parallels suggest that minority parents can provide important insight in how literacy should be taught.

In what ways can the teachers meet the challenge of being culturally responsive to minority parents' perspectives and address the different expectations of culturally diverse students and their families? The Chinese example suggests that minority parents' perspectives on literacy instruction should be seen as an integral part of the minority culture. This view enables teachers to rethink the role of minority parents in literacy education and to incorporate minority perspectives throughout the process of instructional planning and practices.

Rethinking the Role of Minority Parents in Literacy Education

The Chinese parents' covert opposition to school literacy practices also offers a new perspective on school-home power relations, and on the role minority parents can play in their children's literacy development. In Li's (2006) study, though the Chinese parents demonstrated deference to teachers' authority, they challenged the teachers' instructional practice in direct and indirect ways: They requested more homework and more skills-based instruction, and when these requests were not met, they sent their children to private tutoring schools to pursue what they wanted for their children. That is, when their own cultural capital was not accepted and utilized by the school, the parents activated and invested their cultural and economic resources in their children's learning outside school. The parents' actions of pursuing their beliefs outside school suggest that minority parents are not merely contributors, but important decision makers in their children's education.

In order to be culturally responsive, both teachers and parents need to have a deeper understanding of each other's beliefs and practices. Research has revealed that minority parents are often unfamiliar with the teachers' philosophies, and the teachers often do not have a full understanding of minority parents' values and concerns. This lack of mutual understanding often contributes to the misconceptions of each other's literacy practices and leads to cultural conflicts and discontinuities between school and home. There is a need to form a collaborative, two-way communication model so that both teachers and parents can understand the way each defines, values, and uses literacy as part of cultural practices (Cummins, 1989; Harry, 1990; Mapp & Kuttner, 2013). Through such dialogue, both can make adjustments in their practices and work together to improve the children's academic achievement. As Cairney and Munsie (1995) suggest, in a two-way communication model, schooling can be adjusted to meet the needs of families, and parents, in turn, can observe and understand the definitions of literacy that schools support, which ultimately empower individuals to take their place in society.

Incorporating Parents' Perspectives in Literacy Instruction

Gunderson (2001) posits that for meaning-based instruction to work for all students, the voices of all people should be heard. Many mainstream teachers have already implemented many effective literacy approaches that have been proven important to minority students' literacy development (De Jong, Harper, & Coady, 2013; Li, 2006). For example, many have integrated materials across subject areas, used a rich variety of authentic literature, and facilitated students' learning through different activities. These effective practices provide students with opportunities to experiment with and explore literacy and with much-needed exposure to the rich resources of children's literature. Building on these effective practices, teachers can continue to experiment with alternative approaches that incorporate parents' voices in literacy education. Learning from the Chinese parents' perspectives, mainstream teachers may need to address such aspects of instruction as the demand for more explicit instruction and minority parents' bicultural and bilingual expectations.

In terms of direct instruction, teachers need to incorporate *explicit* teaching of reading and writing strategies, vocabulary, and basic skills to better facilitate the development of higher-order thinking skills in students. These strategies are "secrets of reading" or "codes of power" that English language learners need to acquire English literacy (Delpit, 1995; Gersten & Jiménez, 1994). Teachers need to focus on a specific strategy or particular aspect of reading and writing, call to conscious attention what is being taught, and strive to clarify for students the expectations for learning in the contexts of reading and writing (Allington, 1999). That is, teachers can provide students with authentic literacy activities, together with a considerable amount of instruction on specific literacy skills needed for gaining a command of the mainstream discourse (Cambourne, 1999).

In addition to providing explicit instruction, there is also a need to foster bicultural identity and bilingual development. Research has demonstrated that for instruction to be effective for English language learners, it must affirm students' cultural identity and use their first language as a strength (Cummins, 1989; Goldenberg, 2011; Ladson-Billings, 1994; Nieto, 2002). Schools that value students' languages and cultures are often reported to have higher rates of academic success with ESL students (Lucas, Henze, & Donato, 1990; Moll & Diaz, 1993). Monolingual and monocultural practices often not only prevent students from fostering a strategic use of literacy skills from their first language, but also inhibit establishing positive bicultural identity among students (Gersten & Baker, 2000). The exclusion of first language use in the classroom may have serious impact on lower level students' understanding of instruction and interaction with peers and has resulted in their nonparticipation, frustration, and development of negative attitudes toward learning (Wong-Fillmore, 1982). Since cultural identity is related to students' willingness to invest in language learning, there is a need for joint school and home effort to foster students' bicultural and bilingual development to ensure positive learning attitudes.

Research has suggested that there are many ways monolingual mainstream teachers can support linguistic diversity and foster students' positive bicultural and bilingual development (Cummins, 1989; Nieto, 2002). Teachers can do so through developing a culturally responsive curriculum; for example, teachers can select level-appropriate and culturally relevant reading materials so that the students can appreciate the readings and can draw on their own experiences. For learners who struggle with second language literacy, teachers can explore strategies to help these learners to effectively transfer their skills in their first language to their second language. In writing, for example, teachers can allow students to use students' first language vocabulary if they get stuck with words or phrases they cannot express in English.

CONCLUSION

In this chapter, I have provided an interpretation of cross-cultural perspectives on literacy and its instruction and the underlying difference between mainstream teachers and Asian parents through a review of studies on the Chinese population. The findings suggest that literacy instruction in cross-cultural contexts is a complex, multifaceted, and multidimensional process in which different agencies, practices, values, viewpoints, understandings, and ideologies come into play. As Valdés (2001) points out, it is "not a straightforward and unproblematic practice, but a contested site in which there is a struggle about the role and the future of immigrants in our society" (p. 159). Such a process provides us with "a plural conscious-ness in that it requires understanding multiple, often opposing ideas and knowledges, and negotiating these knowledges, not just taking a simple counterstance" (Mohanty, 1991, p. 36).

To conclude, I want to reiterate that the argument for a reconceptual-ization of mainstream cultural models of literacy instruction to take into consideration minority beliefs and perspectives does *not* suggest aban-doning or dismantling the teachers' student-centered instruction to the other end of the pendulum. Rather, I propose that teachers and schools give thoughtful consideration to the implementation of mainstream prac-tices (such as whole-language approaches) in light of the social, cultural, and linguistic needs of the English language learners (Reyes, 1992; Willis, 1995). With some refinement and restructuring, mainstream teachers can strengthen their pedagogical practices and increase the minority students' chances of success with meaning-based literacy instruction (Gersten & Jiménez, 1994). As Gee (1996) asserts,

> The teacher can, at the right time, in the midst of the student's ongoing practice within the culture, and with culturally relevant materials in the class-room, point to the relevant data, focus on the student's attention to the rel-evant aspects of experience that will make the system, the network of cultural models, begin to gel. (p. 91)

REFERENCES

Anderson, J. (1995). Listening to parents' voices: Cross-cultural perceptions of learning to read and write. *Reading Horizons, 35,* 394–413.

Anderson, J., & Gunderson, L. (1997). Literacy from a multicultural perspective. *The Reading Teacher, 50*(6), 514–516.

Au, K. H. (1998). Constructivist approaches, phonics, and the literacy learning of students of students of diverse background. In T. Shanahan & F. V. Rodriguez-Brown (Eds.), *47th Yearbook of the National Reading Conference* (pp. 1–21). Chicago, IL: National Reading Conference.

Au, K. H. (2001). Culturally responsive instruction as a dimension of new literacies. *Reading Online, 5*(1). Retrieved from http://www.readingonline.org/newliteracies/lit_index.asp?HREF=/newliteracies/xu/index.html

Bakhtin, M. M. (1981). *The dialogic imagination: Four essays by M. M. Bakhtin.* Austin, TX: University of Texas Press.

Bomer, R. (1998). Transactional heat and light: More explicit literacy learning. *Language Arts, 76*(1), 11–26.

Cairney, T. H., & Munsie, L. (1995). Parent participation in literacy learning. *The Reading Teacher, 48,* 392–403.

Cambourne, B. (1999). Conditions for literacy learning: Explicit and systematic teaching of reading—a new slogan? *The Reading Teacher, 53*(2), 126–127.

Carless, D. R. (1998). A case study of curriculum implementation in Hong Kong. *System, 26*(1998), 353–368.

Carron, G., & Châu, T. G. (1996). *The quality of primary schools in different developmental contexts.* Paris, France: UNESCO.

Chall, J. S. (1996). *Learning to read: The great debate* (3rd ed.). New York, NY: McGraw Hill.

Chall, J. S. (2000). *The academic achievement challenge.* New York, NY: The Guilford Press.

Chao, R. K. (1996) Chinese and European American mothers' beliefs about the role of parenting in children's school success. *Journal of Cross-Cultural Psychology, 27*(4), 403–423.

Corson, D. J. (1992). Minority cultural values and discourse norms in majority culture classrooms. *The Canadian Modern Language Review, 48*, 472–496.

Cummins, J. (1989). *Empowering minority students.* Sacramento, CA: CA Association for Bilingual Education.

D'Andrade, R., & Strauss, C. (Eds.). (1992). *Human motives and cultural models.* Cambridge, MA: Cambridge University Press.

De Jong, E. J., Harper, C. A., & Coady, M. (2013). Enhanced knowledge and skills for elementary mainstream teachers of English language learners. *Theory into Practice, 52*(2), 89–97.

Delpit, L. D. (1988). The silenced dialogue: Power and pedagogy in educating other people's children. *Harvard educational review, 58*(3), 280–298.

Delpit, L. (1995). *Other people's children: Cultural conflict in the classroom.* New York, NY: The New Press.

Gallimore, R., & Goldenberg, C. (2001). Analyzing cultural models and settings to connect minority achievement and school improvement research. *Educational Psychologist, 36*(1), 45–56.

Gambrell, L. B., & Mazzoni, S. A. (1999). Principles of best practice: Finding the common ground. In L. B. Gambrell, L. M. Morrow, S. B. Neuman, & M. Pressley (Eds.), *Best practices in literacy instruction* (pp. 11–21). New York, NY: Guilford Press.

Gee, J. P. (1996). *Social linguistics and literacies: Ideology in Discourses.* London, UK: Taylor & Francis.

Gee, J. P. (1999). *An introduction to discourse analysis: Theory and method.* London, UK: Routledge.

Gersten, R. M., & Baker, S. (2000). What we know about effective instructional practices for English language learners. *Exceptional Children, 66*(4), 454–470.

Gersten, R. M., & Jiménez, R. T. (1994). A delicate balance: Enhancing literacy instruction for students of English as a second language. *The Reading Teacher, 47*(6), 438–449.

Goldenberg, C. N. (1987). Low-income Hispanic parents' contributions to their first-grade children's word-recognition skills. *Anthropology and Education Quarterly, 18*, 149–179.

Goldenberg, C., & Gallimore, R. (1995). Immigrant Latino parents' values and beliefs about their children's education: Continuities and discontinuities across cultures and generations. In M. Maehr & P. R. Pintrich (Eds.), *Advances in motivation and achievement* (Vol. 9, pp. 183–228). Greenwich, CT: JAI.

Goldenberg, C. (2011). Reading instruction for English language learners. In M. Kamil, P. D. Pearson, E. Moje, & P. Afflerbach (Eds.), *Handbook of Reading Research* (Vol. IV, pp. 684–710). Newark, DE: International Reading Association.

Gunderson, L. (1997). Whole language approaches to reading and writing. In S. Stahl & D. Hayes (Eds.), *Instructional models in reading* (pp. 221–247). Norwood, NJ: Erlbaum.

Gunderson, L. (2001). Different cultural views of whole language. In S. Boran & B. Comber (Eds.), *Critiquing whole language and classroom inquiry* (pp. 242–271). Urbana, IL: National Council of Teachers of English.

Harry, B. (1992). An ethnographic study of cross-cultural communication with Puerto Rican-American families in the special education system. *American Educational Research Journal, 29*(3), 471–494.

Heath, S. B. (1983). *Ways with words: language, life, and work in communities and classrooms.* New York, NY: Cambridge University Press.

Holland, D., & Quinn, N. (1987). *Cultural models of language and thought.* New York, NY: Cambridge University Press.

Huntsinger, C. S., Jose, P. E., Larson, S. L., Kreig, D. B., & Shaligram, C. (2000). Mathematics, vocabulary, and reading development in Chinese American and European American children over primary school years. *Journal of Educational Psychology, 92*, 745–760.

Huntsinger, C. S., Jose, P. E., Rudden, D., Luo, Z., & Kreig, D. B. (2001). Cultural differences in interactions around mathematics tasks in Chinese American and Europe American families. In C. Clark, A. L. Goodwin, & S. J. Lee (Eds.), *Research on the Education of Asian and Pacific Americans* (pp. 75–103). Greenwich, CT: Information Age.

Ladson-Billings, G. (1994). *The dream keepers: Successful teachers of African American children.* San Francisco, CA: Jossey-Bass.

Ladson-Billings, G. (1995). But that's just good teaching! The case for culturally relevant pedagogy. *Theory Into Practice, 34*(3), 159–165.

Langer, J. A. (Ed.). (1987). *Language and literacy and culture: Issues of society and schooling.* Norwood, NJ: Ablex.

Lazar, A. M., & Weisberg, R. (1996). Inviting parents' perspectives: Building home-school partnerships to support children who struggle with literacy. *The Reading Teacher, 50*(3), 228–237.

Li, G. (2002). *"East is East, West is West"? Home literacy, culture, and schooling.* New York, NY: Peter Lang.

Li, G. (2003). Literacy, culture, and politics of schooling: Counternarratives of a Chinese Canadian family. *Anthropology & Education Quarterly, 34*(2), 184–206.

Li, G. (2004). Perspectives on struggling English language learners: Case studies of two Chinese-Canadian children. *Journal of Literacy Research, 36*(1), 29–70.

Li, G. (2006). *Culturally contested pedagogy: Battles of literacy and schooling between mainstream teachers and Asian immigrant parents.* Albany, NY: SUNY Press.

Lucas, T., Henze, R., & Donato, R. (1990). Promoting the success of Latino language-minority students: An exploratory study of six high schools. *Harvard Educational Review, 60*(3), 315–340.

Mapp, K. L., & Kuttner, P. J. (2013). *Partners in education: A dual capacity-building framework for family-school partnerships.* Washington, DC: SEDL and U.S. Department of Education.

Mohanty, C. T. (1991). Introduction: Cartographies of struggle: Third world women and politics of feminism. In C. T. Mohanty, A. Russo, & L. Torres (Eds.), *Third world women and the politics of feminism* (pp. 1–47). Bloomington, IN: Indiana University Press.

Moll, L. C., & Diaz, S. (1993). Change as the goal of educational research. In E. Jacob & C. Jordan (Eds.), *Minority education: Anthropological perspectives* (pp. 67–82). Norwood, NJ: Ablex.

Morris, P., & Lo, M. L. (2000). Shaping the curriculum: Contexts and cultures. *School Leadership & Management, 20*(2), 175–188.

Morrow, L. M., & Gambrell, L. B. (2011). *Best practices in literacy instruction* (4th ed.). New York, NY: Guilford Press.

Nieto, S. (2002). *Language, culture, and teaching: Critical perspectives for a new century.* Mahwah, NJ: Lawrence Erlbaum.

Ogbu, J. U. (1982). Cultural discontinuities and schooling. *Anthropology & Education Quarterly, 13*(4), 290–307.

Peng, S. S., & Wright, D. (1994). Explanation of academic achievement of Asian American students. *The Journal of Educational Research, 87*(6), 346–352.

Reyes, M. de la Luz. (1991). A process approach to literacy using dialogue journals and literature logs with second language learners. *Research in the Teaching of English, 25*(3), 291–313.

Reyes, M. de la Luz. (1992). Challenging venerable assumptions: Literacy instruction for linguistically different students. *Harvard Educational Review, 62,* 427–446.

Schieffelin, B. B. (1986). Introduction. In B. B. Schieffelin & P. Gilmore (Eds.), *The acquisition of literacy: Ethnographic perspectives.* Norwood, NJ: Ablex.

Siu, S. F. (1994). Taking no chances: A profile of a Chinese-American family's support for school success. *Equity and Choice 10*(2), 23–32.

Spiegel, D. L. (1992). Blending whole language and systematic direct instruction. *The Reading Teacher, 46*(1), 38–44.

Spradley, J. P., & McCurdy, D. W. (Eds.). (2011). *Conformity and conflict: Readings in cultural anthropology* (14th ed.). New York, NY: Pearson.

Stevenson, H. W., Lee, S., & Mu, X. (2013). Successful achievement in mathematics: China and the United States. In P. Heymans & C. Lieshout (Eds.), *Developing talent across the lifespan* (pp. 167-181). Sussex, UK: Psychology Press.

Strauss, C. (1992). Models and motives. In R. G. D'Andrade & C. Strauss (Eds.), *Human motives and cultural models* (pp. 1–20). Cambridge, MA: Cambridge University Press.

Street, B. (1993). Introduction: The new literacy studies. In B. Street (Ed.), *Cross-cultural approaches to literacy* (pp. 1–22). New York, NY: Cambridge University Press.

Townsend, J. S., & Fu, D. (1998). A Chinese boy's joyful initiation into American literacy. *Language Arts, 75*(3), 193–201.

Valdés, G. (1996). *Con Respeto:Bridging the distance between culturally diverse families and schools: An ethnographic portrait.* New York, NY: Teachers College Press.

Valdés, G. (2001). *Learning and not learning English: Latino students in American schools.* New York, NY: Teachers College Press.

Wells, G. (1998). Some questions about direct instruction: Why? To whom? How? And when? *Language Arts, 76*(1), 27–35.

Wertsch, J. V. (1991). *Voices of the mind: A socio-cultural approach to mediated action.* Cambridge, MA: Harvard University Press.

Wong-Fillmore, L. (1982). Language minority students and school participation: What kind of English is needed? *Journal of Education, 164*(2), 143–156.

Wharton-McDonald, R., Pressley, M., & Hampston, J. M. (1998). Literacy instruction in nine first-grade classrooms: Teacher characteristics and student achievement. *The Elementary School Journal, 99*(2), 101–128.

Willis, A. I. (1995). Reading the world of school literacy: Contextualizing the experience of a young African American male. *Harvard Educational Review, 65*(1), 30–49.

Xu, H. (1999). Young Chinese ESL children's home literacy experiences. *Reading Horizons, 40*(1), 47–64.

Zhang, S. Y., & Carrasquillo, A. (1995). Chinese parents' influence on academic performance. *New York State Association for Bilingual Education Journal 10*, 46–53.

Zhang, C., Ollila, L. O., & Harvey, C. B. (1998). Chinese parents' perceptions of their children's literacy and schooling in Canada. *Canadian Journal of Education, 23*(2), 182–190.

CHAPTER 7

WHY ARE THE SPANISH SPEAKERS IN THE BACK OF THE ROOM IN A DUAL IMMERSION SETTING?

Marisol Ruiz

INTRODUCTION

Literacy engagement is supported as effective strategy for boosting fluency in bilingual multiliteracy contexts in an elementary school in southern New Mexico. A qualitative study of the effects of integrating ELLs into regular bilingual instruction shows that students in both languages are more eager to participate and willing to express themselves in both languages used, regardless of fluency level. This result is achieved in spite of the negative context of the limited time and distractions of the testing requirements of NCLB for teachers and students.

Immigration and Schooling: Redefining the 21st Century America, pp. 125–138
Copyright © 2015 by Information Age Publishing

BILINGUAL EDUCATION EFFORTS IN
THE TESTING FRENZY CONTEXT

Gándara and Orfield (2010) wrote an eye-opening piece on how the U.S. is returning to segregation, especially segregating Latino English language learners (ELLs) who, in the testing frenzy, have been segregated even further. National Assessment of Educational Progress (NAEP) scores show that states—New Mexico and Texas, for example—that allow bilingual education have less of an achievement gap between ELLs and monolingual English speakers than states—such as California, Arizona, and Massachusetts—with English-only instruction policies (Gándara & Orfield, 2010). This does not mean that Texas and New Mexico do not have achievement gaps. In fact, Rumberger and Tran (2010) showed that more than offering bilingual education, what determines the achievement gap is how segregated ELLs are. They conclude that the more we integrate ELLs, the less of an achievement gap we will have. This is not to say that bilingual education does not work, because the research shows that it does (Baker, 2006; Cadiero-Kaplan, 2004; Gándara & Hopkins, 2010; Garcia, 2009; Izquierdo, 2011). The most pertinent question, then, becomes: Which bilingual model best helps integrate ELL students with dominant English speakers? The answer is the dual immersion program, where students who are monolingual in English and Spanish come together to share their language base knowledge.

In New Mexico, where the largest ethnic population is Chicano/Latino who speak different degrees of Spanish, bilingual education is a must. According to the 2010 U.S. Census, New Mexico's Chicano/Latino population is 46.3% of their total, making it the largest ethnic group in the state, followed by Caucasians at 27.9%, and Native Americans at 9%. New Mexico is a minority majority state, with 72% of the population being people of color. The preadolescent population in public schools K–12 shows that the Chicano/Latino population is increasing, with 57% of the total, followed by Caucasians at 29%, Native Americans 11%, Asians 1%, and African Americans 2% (New Mexico Public Education Department, 2010). This growth is reflected in preschool populations: the Chicano/Latino is measured at 62%, followed by Caucasians at 21%, Native Americans 14%, African Americans 2%, and Asians 1% (NMPED, 2010). Bilingual education comes naturally to a state that has bilingual education as part of its constitution.

New Mexico was the first state to pass a bilingual education law in the United States with the Bilingual Multicultural Education Act (NMPED, 2010). At first, as in other states that passed similar laws, bilingual education was used to teach English. New Mexico, in an effort to be true to its bilingual Native American language roots, passed a resolution in 1989 called "English Plus," aimed at invigorating the bilingual education law. In

2004, New Mexico passed the Bilingual Education Act, the goal of which is to ensure that students in the bilingual programs will become bilingual and biliterate. New Mexico, in implementing this law, is committed to helping children become bilingual.

However, even with the program's success with English learners, monolingual English speakers, Native Americans, and Chicano/Latino (see NMPED, 2010), students are not enrolling in bilingual programs. In 2009, only 17% of the public school student population participated in these programs. Of that 17%, 78% were Chicano/Latino, 15% Native American, and 7% other (NMPED). Seventeen percent of New Mexico school population is considered to be English language learners (ELLs). Not all ELLs enroll in bilingual programs.

With the passage of the No Child Left Behind Act (NCLB) in 2001 and its mandate that by 2014, all students must be proficient in reading and math, the Bilingual Education Act was eliminated and replaced by "scientifically based reading methods." NCLB instituted two reading initiatives, Reading First and Early Reading First. For this study, we reviewed the mandated methods of Reading First, which are phonemic awareness, phonics, vocabulary, fluency, and comprehension. If educators use these methods, NCLB leads us to believe, the achievement gap will close and reading scores will rise. This, however, is not what has happened; in fact, the NAEP test scores have remained stagnant in reading and math (Ravitch, 2010). Small gains have occurred in reading in the elementary grades, but by high school any modest improvement has disappeared (Ravitch, 2010). Ravitch argued that there were states, such as Texas, that have inflated their scores, but the NAEP was able to detect the discrepancies and show that Texas scores were flat like all other states in the country.

In New Mexico, ELLs must take the New Mexico English Language Proficiency Assessment (NMELPA) authored by Pearson. The NMELPA has five different categories: beginning, early intermediate, intermediate, early advanced, and advanced. In 2009, 18% of ELLs scored advanced, 48% early advanced, 23% intermediate, 6% early intermediate, and 3% beginning (NMPED, 2010). According to NMELPA, ELLs in New Mexico are making progress; however, only 18% were considered English proficient and are no longer required to take the test. In 2010, New Mexico changed the assessment to measure English proficiency from NMELPA to Assessing Comprehension and Communication in English State to State (ACCESS).

Adequate yearly progress (AYP) in New Mexico has declined from 45.9% in 2006 to 23% in 2010 (NMPED, 2010). Ravitch (2010) showed that the number of schools not meeting AYP increased nationwide. Furthermore, Ravitch explained that AYP is impossible to achieve, because each year the schools are asked to increase their points. In many ways schools are punished, even if they had a small increase.

The Testing Frenzy

The testing frenzy stands in the way of developing bilingual programs. It is not the tests per se; it is how they are being implemented and how administrators are interpreting the scores. The National Academy of Education cautioned people about the NAEP because it focused on writing, reading, and math (Ravitch, 2010). Education is more than just these three skills. However, with NCLB, New Mexico schools are increasing the number of tests children take. New Mexico students in the third to fifth grade are tested with New Mexico Standards Based Assessment (NMSBA) in reading and math, taken two hours a day for seven days; tests in English, Dynamic Indicators of Basic Early Literacy Skills (DIBELS) and Spanish, Indicadores Dinámiocos del Exito en la Lectura (IDEL), are used to monitor their reading skills; the Developmental Reading Assessment (DRA) test garnering additional information on reading is taken three times a year; the test, Measures of Academic Progress (MAP), is a computerized formative assessment taken three times a year. The NMSBA can be taken in Spanish for three consecutive years, and there is an additional two-year waiver that schools and students can apply for. Even though districts say the DRA and DIBELS/IDEL tests are optional, most schools conduct them anyway as a way of covering their backs. Bilingual students, in addition to the four tests mentioned, must take four additional exams: ACCESS, to determine English language proficiency; IDEL, to measure their Spanish reading skills over time; IDEA Proficiency Test (IPT), to measure Spanish language proficiency; and ELD2, to measure students' Spanish reading, which is taken three times a year. Once they pass ACCESS and IPT, students are no longer required to take the exam. However, they will continue to take ELD2. Bilingual students will take IDEL from K–3rd grade. In the school, we observed that teachers allowed the whole morning for students to complete NMSBA, which took nine days, but some students did not stop testing until long after the time allotted had expired. What is the point in going to school if tests are being taken as the sole truth about a child's ability?

State legislators, who are dictating how teachers should teach or are forcing districts to suffer consequences for not following orders, have made the teaching profession more stressful. New Mexico's Governor Martinez recently signed executive order 2011–024, which creates the New Mexico Effective Teaching Task Force. The task force is researching the effectiveness of evaluating teachers based on students' test scores with merit pay awarded to those teachers whose students have high scores. If passed into law, teachers will need less and less incentive to teach anything but a test in order to increase their scores. Furthermore, this kind of legislation will force teachers to continue to focus on top-down curriculum rather than the joy of teaching and learning.

Testing experts and companies have also advised caution in making important decisions on a child's future solely on the basis of a test (Ravitch, 2010). Kumashiro (2008) argued that standardized tests are culturally biased. They are based on white middle-class responses—if the correct response is not achieved, then the question is dropped from the test. Further, Kumashiro has argued that tests are assimilation tools, where the more one can assimilate, the higher the student can score. In New Mexico, rain rarely occurs, and the sun shines nearly every day; but when students are asked "what do you use the umbrella for?" all of them will respond: "to protect me from the sun." In standardized testing this is incorrect because the correct answer is to protect them from the rain; but in a place where rain rarely comes, especially because when drought is in full swing, students use the umbrellas only to protect themselves against the sun. The increased testing of New Mexico's bilingual students does not help bilingual programs thrive, especially in their mission of becoming biliterate.

NCLB mandates of Reading First also help to assimilate but are in conflict with the state's effort to protect bilingualism. Under the mandate of Reading First, school districts purchased scripted curriculum that all teachers would use to drill their students with its "scientifically based reading methods." Reading First is based on the research conducted by the National Reading Panel.

It is unfortunate, as Coles (2007) pointed out in his research on the National Reading Panel, that "skills emphasis instruction is not a superior method to teaching skills as needed" (p. 42); students learn skills in literature-based instruction, the same as in skills-focused instruction, and "skills emphasis instruction is not superior to whole language teaching. Moreover, the research used in the report of the National Reading Panel, on the contrary, indicates that whole language elicits a more positive attitude and more enthusiasm for reading as skills-emphasis teaching would.

The analysis by Coles (2007), besides casting doubts on the veracity of the conclusions reached in that research, demonstrated that the research itself is inconclusive and does not support the scientifically based reading methods proposed by this legislation. Yet it is now the case that, in New Mexico, some legislators are hindering bilingual education by mandating that future teachers take a test based on reading methods not supported by research. Coles (2003) takes a dim view of this stance that may smack of vested interests. These legislators are making it easier for corporations to produce materials based on these methods rather than a literacy engagement model, which would entail the corporations being invovled in the community and with children before they produced any curriculum. Literacy engagement has been proven to work, and it is an effective method to use with bilingual education students, as Cummins (2009) and Krashen (2004) have pointed out. Literacy engagement aims at getting the child interested in learning. When children are engaged, they are happy; they are learning with joy, as they are self-motivated to continue to research and to learn outside of school.

The New Mexico Bilingual Multicultural Education Programs annual report (NMPED, 2010) presents a number of suggestions for improving their bilingual programs. Many bilingual programs in the state and country would agree with these recommendations in order to improve their bilingual programs. I've chosen the ones that pertain to what I saw in our study.

1. Instruction:
    a. District staff and administrators must receive professional development in order to implement best practices and models for bilingual students.
    b. Teachers must implement strategies where they do not translate from language in home and instructional language.
    c. There needs to be equal allocation of time used in language arts in the second language
    d. More rigorous academic expectations in the second language.

2. Instructional Materials: Teachers need to have more instructional materials in the home language.
3. Parent Notification: Parents must be notified of their children's progress in the bilingual program and they must be informed about bilingual education and how it can enhance their children's learning opportunities.
4. School System Climate: The school must be supportive of bilingual programs and students as they are developing English and their home language.
5. Staffing: There is a shortage of bilingual TESOL teachers.

I highlighted these five needs for improvement of New Mexico bilingual programs because these are the issues that we noticed in Estrellita Elementary school, which is located in southern New Mexico.

ESTRELLITA ELEMENTARY

This qualitative study took place in a southern New Mexico school named Estrellita Elementary (a pseudonym). Estrellita Elementary is a small dual immersion and English-only school with a student body of 267 students. They have two classrooms for each grade level. One classroom is dual immersion; the other is monolingual English instruction. The student body is 88% Hispanic, 10.1% Caucasian; 87% are considered economically disadvantaged, 30% are designated as being English language learners (ELLs), and 24% are in special education. More than half of the school is either ELL or in special education. The ELL students are in bilingual classrooms. In this study, we worked with 126 students who were in third to fifth grade.

The purpose of this qualitative study was to implement multiliteracy practices in third to fifth grade classrooms. There were six classrooms for each grade level, three bilingual and three monolingual. Our intention was to add to the scripted literacy curriculum. Preservice teachers were trained on how to implement multiliteracy practices with students. There were four preservice student teachers in each classroom. Over the course of a semester, they entered the third to fifth grade classrooms two hours a week to implement bilingual multiliteracy practices. The bilingual multiliteracy project implemented dialogue journals, Readers Theater, critical dialogue, philosophy, drawing, writing their own stories, photography, and filming. We worked with the children from January to April. In April, teachers needed the week before testing to go over possible testing questions. April was testing month.

No Longer Dual Immersion but Transition

As part of the No Child Left Behind legislation, students are tested in third grade. Even though students are in third grade, those who have not passed the English proficiency test will take the state test in Spanish, NMSBA.

One of the things we noticed at Estrellita Elementary was that by the third grade, the dual immersion model had been abandoned. The model that was being used was transitional to a certain extent. However, since the students did not pass the English proficiency test, they were required to take the NMSBA exam in Spanish. Therefore, they were put at a table in the back of the room in order to prepare them for the exam. The other children in all three bilingual classrooms referred to them as the "Spanish group." All of the students had been in the dual immersion program in kindergarten, but it had ended by third grade. The teacher mostly spoke English, and every morning, teachers prepared them for the exam. Teachers spent the year trying to prepare students to do well in the exam.

The Spanish Group

The Spanish groups in all three classrooms were not only practicing their reading and comprehension skills in Spanish, but they were also in the lowest reading level. Other students noticed them and did not make fun of them; they just viewed them as the Spanish group and the lowest reading level. They were viewed by others and themselves as academically low achievers.

The author of this chapter and the preservice teachers noticed that students in the Spanish group in all three classrooms were put at a table in a rear corner of the classrooms. This separated them from the group of bilingual students who had passed the English proficiency exam and were in the higher levels of reading. The classes were conducted solely in English, and the teacher did give instruction in Spanish, but just so the Spanish group could complete their test-preparation work in Spanish. The mornings were spent preparing students for reading tests and filling out workbooks. Students completed Response to Intervention (RTI) and workbooks of the scripted curriculum. The Spanish students worked in Spanish; the rest worked in English. During Spanish week, the third grade teacher tried to have whole group activities in Spanish. Fourth and fifth grades continued using English and Spanish only for the Spanish group.

Implementation of the Bilingual Multiliteracy Project

Preservice teachers in each of the grade levels implemented culturally relevant literature accompanied by critical and philosophical discussions preservice student teachers created as future professionals. In third grade, they began to read *The Girl From Chimel/La niña de Chimel* by Rigoberta Menchú (2000); in fourth grade they read *The Circuit/Cajas de Carton* (1996), by Francisco Jimenez; and in fifth grade they read *And the Earth Did Not Devour Them/Y no se lo trago la tierra* (1987) by Thomas Rivera. One of the first things that the author of this chapter and preservice teachers noticed was that when students in "Spanish group" read in English, they lowered their voice, and as they dialogued about the story, they spoke in a louder, more confident voice. Students in the scripted reading curriculum were placed in different grade-level readings. The Spanish group knew they were the lowest reading level. Therefore, they did not feel confident in their reading skills in English; however, they were confident in their oral skills, and dialogue allowed them to find their voice. They were confident speaking in English and Spanish. At the Spanish table we implemented what Ofelia Garcia (2009) called *translanguaging*. Translanguaging strategy supports the idea that students do not turn off one language and then turn on the next. Students read in Spanish and dialogued and wrote in English or read in English and dialogued and wrote in Spanish. One of the things that all of us noticed was that when the students spoke, they had a hard time sticking to one language—they would begin to speak in Spanish and, then, revert to English and vice versa.

Whole Group: Integration

One of the reasons we did whole group books was to stop tracking students. Preservice teachers were pushed to integrate rather than continue to segregate the "Spanish group." One of the things they noticed right away as they integrated the groups was that students in both groups began to use both languages. In whole-group discussions, students discussed their stories using both languages.

Preservice teachers began to notice that the students who were not confident in reading English began to read with more confidence. They also noticed that the students who felt they could not speak Spanish used it in order to express themselves. In whole group, preservice teachers said they felt they needed to encourage the students to use both languages. They felt that they had rebuilt their self-esteem by telling stories about themselves and how lucky they were to be bilingual. One preservice teacher told her students in Spanish, "I also had a hard time reading and I did not want anyone to hear me because I thought I was not speaking, but I did it because I wanted to be better. It took time but you can do it too."

Another had to tell her bilingual students who passed the English exam that being bilingual was something to be proud of when they did not want to write or read in Spanish. The preservice teacher asked the students why they did not want to write or speak in Spanish, and they responded that they did not want to. She spoke in English and said: "I am bilingual, and I still have to develop my Spanish, so I practice it to be better. Being bilingual is beautiful because it is part of our culture and we want to be able to talk to more people than just those who speak one language." It was through the preservice teachers talking and encouraging them to be bilingual that students began to speak more openly in both languages. Other preservice student teachers just had to say: "Look at me, I am bilingual and I love being bilingual" for children to want to be like them. They would respond: "I am bilingual too, you know." The children were happy to identify with their young preservice teachers.

The classroom's teachers told a different story: The students' parents no longer wanted their children in bilingual education, but to be taught in English. This is why they had to teach in English, and the only students who were taught in Spanish were at the table in the back of the room because they had not yet passed the English proficiency exam. As a result, the combination of the Spanish table at the back of the room, parents wanting their children to be in English only classrooms, and teachers conducting their classes in English, students looked at Spanish as the ugly step child. The students who had not passed the exam continued to view themselves as lacking the skills necessary to read in English, and therefore, feared to read in English or feared to write in English and feared being told once again it is not good enough.

Apparently, we have not learned from the countless stories of students not doing well on tests but turning out to be geniuses, as in Victor Villaseñor's memoir, *Burro Genius* (2004). These tests continue to perpetuate the deficit in our children, especially our bilingual children. Teachers dread the possibility that the students might not pass the exam, so they spend countless hours trying to prepare their students to pass the exam.

Measuring Happiness

In our project, we did not test the students we observed but evaluated the project by asking students themselves if they liked the activity. All classrooms' teachers and preservice teachers mentioned that students were happy while engaged in the literacy activity where they wrote their own books, read stories, dialogued, acted pieces of the story, filmed, and reviewed their own acting. When the students saw their acting, all they did was laugh at their acting skills. Preservice teachers mentioned over and over again how children in their classrooms begged to act out the story again. Readers Theater is not just good for fluency, but also for comprehension and engaging children in literacy. Once students acted the story, they discussed it. How do we measure happiness? Laughter? Now that I mentioned this issue, will someone develop a test to measure it? The point that we are trying to make is that we cannot measure everything. How does one measure the joy of learning?

After the project was completed, the students returned to RTI and reading the books scripted for their different grade levels. Did they resist? Yes, during RTI, the children begged to read the books with language that meant something, language that was alive and not dead. Preservice teachers asked the classroom teacher if they could continue to read the books we brought in instead of the Reading Street. Teachers were nice enough to allow it, but we disrupted their routine and this did not make them happy, but the children were happy. Fourth graders read the third grade book *The Girl from Chimel*. The students were not as lucky when they asked and begged to continue to conduct Readers Theater. Testing was near, and Readers Theater must wait because bilingual students were being tested for English proficiency and NMSBA was going to begin in a week.

After students had experienced the literature we had provided, they were able to engage in critical literacy and see that the books they were being forced to read really did not have a detailed story line. One student commented on *The Circuit:* "I like the book because there is drama, something is always going to happen, and those books are boring." Reading

Street scripted reading curriculum books were not novels; they did not have a story line full of excitement to follow.

Another point that made students happy was the interaction with the whole class on the reading, not just within their reading level. Students were able to engage together in their different reading levels. They discussed the book together, sharing their ideas and thoughts on the book. This made the Spanish group happy because they were no longer segregated at the back of the room but incorporated into the whole class; Spanish was given its place at the table as a valuable skill, and students were able to discuss the story in both languages.

Because of NCLB, schools are racing to reach AYP by 2014 while students are being segregated and tracked within each classroom into English/ Spanish and reading levels. In all three classes, students who did not pass the English proficiency exam were also considered the lowest readers. NCLB has caused some schools to abandon the dual immersion model by third grade so students can pass the exams, which are in English. Children who pass the NMELPA (now ACCESS) are required to take the exam in English schools, and the ones who do not can take it in Spanish at a segregated table where they are the only ones who receive most of their instruction in Spanish. Teachers want their students to pass the exam so they resort to teaching solely in English, with Spanish used for the Spanish group.

Students are tracked because of their reading level, making children in low reading levels feel they cannot read and are not smart. In all three bilingual classes, the Spanish group in the back of the room was the "lowest level" of readers in English. Third to fifth graders are segregated at tables in the back of the room if they did not pass the English proficiency exam. At those tables, students are drilled for hours with the scripted reading curriculum in Spanish because they will take the exam in Spanish. Because students seated at the Spanish table are usually also the lowest readers, they begin to fear English. This arrangement causes fear and anxiety in students during reading and writing English, but not in speaking. Unfortunately, the school did not have a parents' night where bilingual education was explained.

CONCLUSION

If New Mexico is going to be a leader in bilingual education, the state must abandon Reading First mandates because they are not conducive to fostering bilingualism. In fact they are conducive to an English only agenda (Gutierrez, 2007). As Garcia (2009) pointed out, in English some students learn to read through letter sounds (phonics), but in Spanish students learn to read through syllables. By instituting Reading First, the state of New Mexico has already given preference to an English-only agenda. Districts need to stop buying scripted curriculum because no one program is the miracle pill. One size does not fit all (Gutierrez, 2007; Janks, 2010). We must create curriculum that respects and honors local knowledge (González, Moll, & Amanti, 2005).

The literacy engagement model should be implemented so teachers become professional creators of lessons and curricula that engage children to love to learn. If students are engaged in literacy, they will succeed academically (Allington, 2002a, 2002b; Cummins, 2009; Guthrie, 2004; Krashen, 2004).

Pacing guides are not conducive to learning. Students need to be given time to learn. We cannot mandate that students learn faster. Students need time to ponder ideas, to create their book as authors of literacy, not solely as consumers. Multiliteracy practices must be implemented in bilingual classrooms because they help to motivate, excite, and engage students in multiple ways to engage in literacy. At a national level, we must abandon NCLB requirements because they have driven the love for, and excitement out of, learning. Teachers in their quest to pass the test water down the curriculum so students will pass the test (Irvine & Larson, 2007). At the state level, if we want to continue to be a state that honors bilinguals, we must abandon NCLB as it pushes schools into English-only models because after five years students must take the test in English. In addition, students who score proficient before those five years are then put in the English part of the classroom where they receive most of their instruction in English in order for them to pass this test. This is a disservice to students and families who are in bilingual public schools because they want to be bilingual and biliterate. The testing frenzy must stop. If tests are the most important tool in this educational system, then why do we have schools and teachers, if students' class work and teachers' professional opinion do not count?

Research on tracking demonstrates how it affects children's self-esteem and how they view themselves as learners (Oakes, 1985). Students need to stop being tracked and segregated into different reading levels. Our research demonstrates how bilingual students in the lowest reading level did not view themselves as academically capable of succeeding. If students do not pass the English proficiency exam, we cannot segregate them but must continue to integrate them into a dual bilingual immersion model where Spanish-speaking students will learn from those who are more fluent in English and those whose native language is English will learn from those who are more fluent in Spanish. Integration of the Spanish table will help students develop their English, and the dominant English speakers will develop their Spanish. This has been proven to be a successful bilingual model (Izquierdo, 2011).

REFERENCES

Allington, R. (2002a). *Big Brother and the national reading curriculum.* Portsmouth, NH: Heinemann.

Allington,R; L. {2002b). You can't learn much from books you can't read. *Educational Leadership, 60*(3), 16–19.

Baker, C. (2006). *Foundations of bilingual education and bilingualism* (4th ed.). Clevedon, UK: Multilingual Matters.

Cadiero-Kaplan, K. (2004). *The literacy curriculum & bilingual education.* New York, NY: Peter Lang.

Coles, G. (2003). *Reading the naked truth: Literacy, legislation, and lies.* Portsmouth, NH: Heinemann.

Coles, G. (2007). Forging "facts" to fit an explanation: How to make reading research support skills emphasis instruction. In J. Larson (Ed.), *Literacy as snake oil* (pp. 27–42). New York, NY: Peter Lang.

Cummins, J. (2009). Transformative multiliteracies pedagogy: School based strategies for closing the achievement gap. *Multiple Voices for Ethnically Diverse Exceptional Learners, 11*(2), 38–56.

Gándara, P., & Hopkins, M. (2010). *English learners and restrictive language policies.* New York, NY: Teachers College Press.

Gándara, P., & Orfield, G. (2010, July 08). A return to the "Mexican Room": The segregation of Arizona's English learners. UCLA: The Civil Rights Project. Retrieved from http://civilrightsproject.ucla.edu/research/k-12-education/language-minority-students/arizona-educational-equity-project-abstracts-and-papers

Garcia, O. (2009). *Bilingual education in the 21ˢᵗ century: A global perspective.* Oxford, UK: Wiley Blackwell.

González, N., Moll, L., & Amanti, C. (2005). *Funds of knowledge: Theorizing practices in households, communities, and classrooms.* Mahwah, NJ: Lawrence Erlbaum Associates.

Guthrie, J. (2004). Teaching for literacy engagement. *Journal of Literacy Research, 36,* 1–30.

Gutierrez, K. (2007). "Sameness as fairness": The new tonic of equality and opportunity. In J. Larson (Ed.), *Literacy as snake oil* (pp. 109–122). New York, NY: Peter Lang.

Irvine, P., & Larson, J. (2007). Literacy packages in practice: Constructing academic disadvantage. In J. Larson (Ed.), *Literacy as snake oil* (pp. 49–72). New York, NY: Peter Lang.

Izquierdo, E. (2011). One supana time ... Children don't know that they know, but they know! *Soleado: Promising Practices From the Field, 4,* 1-11.

Janks, H. (2010). *Literacy and power.* New York, NY: Routledge.

Jimenez, F. (1999). *The circuit: Stories from the life of a migrant child.* Boston, MA: Houghton Mifflin-Harcourt.

Krashen, S. (2004). *The power of reading: Insights from the research* (2nd ed.). Portsmouth, NH: Heinemann.

Kumashiro, K. (2008). *The seduction of common sense: How the right has framed the debate on America's schools.* New York, NY: Teachers College Press.

Menchú, R. (2000). *The girl from the Chime* (David Unger, English Translation, 2003). Toronto, Ontario: Alfagura Infantil.

New Mexico Public Education Department (NMPED)/The Bilingual Multicultural Education Bureau (2010, March 3). *New Mexico Bilingual Multicultural Education Programs Annual Performance Report.* Retrieved from http://www.ped.state.nm.us/div/learn.serv/Bilingual

Oakes, J. (1985). *Keeping track: How schools structure inequality.* New Haven, CT: Yale University Press.

Ravitch, D. (2010). *The death and life of the great American school system: How testing and choice are undermining education.* New York, NY: Basic Books.

Rivera, T. (1987). *And the Earth did not devour him.* New York, NY: Glencoe McGraw-Hill.

Rumberger, R., & Tran, L. (2010). State language policies, school language practices, and the English language learner achievement gap. In P. Gándara & M. Hopkins (Eds.), *English learners and restrictive language policies* (pp. 86–101). New York, NY: Teachers College Press.

Villaseñor, V. (2004). *Burro genius.* New York, NY: HarperCollins.

CHAPTER 8

TEACHING IN THE FACE OF RACE

An Autoethnographical Theoretical Reflection

Barrel Gueye and Catie Lalonde

INTRODUCTION

Social issues in education may be explored broadly in terms of the continuous conversations between schools in society or, more specifically, in relation to the rapport developed within classrooms. This chapter explores how two professors navigate classroom interactions in their individual courses, wherein they and their students investigate critical issues in education.

We are currently educating American and Canadian graduate students (with Canadian students predominating) through the Education Department at a northeastern private Catholic U.S. college. As we engage in conversations with our students about various theoretical issues relating to critical aspects and trends in American education, the race of each instructor becomes a factor in sustaining student interest in these topics.

Immigration and Schooling: Redefining the 21st Century America, pp. 139–150
Copyright © 2015 by Information Age Publishing
All rights of reproduction in any form reserved.

Specifically, when one professor, a Black woman who grew up in Africa, analyzes racial issues, race is seen as "her thing," her area of interest, whereas when the other professor, a White woman originally from the United States, analyzes these same issues, her students talk about her "passion" for the material—not her race. Not only is race and whiteness as an empty signifier implicated in these differing students' responses, but language also plays a part, in relation to speaking English with a foreign accent (as with the first professor) versus speaking "American" English without said accent (as with the second professor). We do not find these responses to be necessarily strange, as many of the predominantly Canadian students are White and highly privileged in terms of *insulated* social class backgrounds. However, in order to attend the college, the Canadian students must cross the U.S.–Canadian border daily, contending with the many questions associated with their identities that such border crossings (Anzaldua, 1987) entail, making this disconnection between their lived experiences and the educational issues discussed in the classroom very odd indeed.

In order to provide a framework for our analysis, we look to bodies of literature exploring critical pedagogy, student-centered teaching and learning (Freire, 1970, 2005; Kincheloe, 2005), identity formation (Anzaldua, 1987; Giroux, 1994), and race and gender issues in teacher education classrooms (Hayes & Groves, 2002; hooks, 1994). By synthesizing issues raised in this research, we construct theoretical grounding for our investigation, as well as examples of other educators who have engaged in similar classroom negotiations.

REVIEW OF THE RELEVANT LITERATURE

Critical pedagogy is mobilized through continuous reflection and action in relation to the classroom—the place where theoretical and practical contexts meet (Freire, 2005). Students must be empowered by problem-posing rather than "banking" concepts of education (Freire, 1970), thereby fueling critical interactions between teachers and students. Further, we must mobilize a sense of urgency in terms of educating for social justice, encouraging our students to turn these critical lenses on their local and global communities, in an effort to resolve structural issues (Kincheloe, 2005). Tate (1997) and Ladson-Billings (1995) focus on the social construction of race, racism, and discrimination through the critical race theory in education. These authors theorize race and address the limitations of the current multicultural paradigm. Race, place, and nation involve continuous "border crossings" (Anzaldua, 1987), whether through physical or psychological movement, and cultural perceptions of representations contribute greatly to how these cultural crossings play out. The "pedagogy of

representation" and "demystifying" representations encourage students—
and teachers—to explore the ways in which meaning is produced through
power structures and how this affects identity construction (Giroux, 1994,
p. 87). Thus, cultural difference is a *relational* issue, rather than one that
isolates and marks groups, making critical examination of cultural images
representing such differences an integral part of the educational—and,
by association, identity formational—process. Hayes and Groves (2002)
provide specific experiences, using movies and video with undergraduate
preservice teachers in their social foundations classrooms, in order to probe
racial issues in education. While also highlighting issues of critical pedagogy in American higher education classrooms, hooks (1994) complicates
power relationships between students and teachers, She views education
as an *actively reflective* practice that emphasizes the whole person and well
being of *both* teachers and students, and her emphasis on educating the
"whole person" suggests a complex approach to both student and teacher
identity formation, as well as to classroom interactions as a whole, exposing
and interrogating power in the American higher education classroom. As
Foucault (1981) has explained at length in relation to sex and sexual identity formation, relationships of power between the dominant (in schools,
teachers are typically coded as such) and resistant (in schools, students are
usually given this label) are local, mobile, and transitory, with the dominant structures depending on patterns to reinforce their power over the
resistant.

The "Critical Issues and Future Trends in Education" course that we
both teach is meant to provide preservice teachers with a grasp of current
educational issues, as well as theoretical approaches to assist in addressing
these issues in their future classrooms. An exact description of the course
is as follows:

> This [course] is designed to give students an in-depth understanding of con-
> temporary issues and future trends in education. Among the specific issues
> discussed are educational inequalities, school choice, standardized testing,
> religion in public schools, school violence, classroom management, and the
> move toward values, character, or moral education. The course also explores
> the larger socio-cultural and political-economic contexts of education and
> schooling.

As this overview suggests, the themes explored in the course run the
gamut of educational issues, exposing students to everything from standardized testing to character education. And, as noted above, theory is an
important focus of this course, requiring students to tackle such foundational theorists as Kincheloe, McLaren, Foucault, and Freire.

One Professor's Classroom Experiences: "If you are not happy, go back to where you come from"

I am a Black woman from Senegal, West Africa and I speak with an accent. I will start by sharing my philosophy of education, which is deeply rooted in my beliefs of education as a means to promote students' and teachers' personal and academic growth. The foundation of my teaching has been to foster development of knowledge; to promote social justice, democracy, equality; but most importantly to encourage students' critical thinking and global awareness.

In my classroom, I always create spaces of dialogue. The class becomes an interactive environment based on a student-centered framework, a learning space nurtured by different but valuable perspectives through the building of a critical way of thinking. As well, I view teaching as an avenue to promote open-mindedness and cultural awareness, where all values and cultures are respected, where students as well as teachers craft their identities through cooperation, tolerance, acceptance, mutual respect, and consideration.

I share the educational philosopher Dewey's view of education that puts the emphasis on the learners who must contribute to the process of acquiring knowledge and whose interests and inclination should be the starting point of the educator's focus. I also value Noddings' vision of humanistic education on the levels of local, national, and global community that promotes appreciation for diversity, encourages empathy with others, and opens the door to a peaceful coexistence of humanity.

However, despite my attempt to create a community of learners (both students and teachers) where education, as hooks put it, becomes "a practice of freedom" and where students' voices are encouraged and challenged, I encountered at times resistance and repulsion. Many of my students felt at ease and welcome to participate in creating safe and accessible spaces for dialogue as long as the issue of race and ethnicity are not the topics of discussion.

I am very much inspired by Freire's progressive vision of education, where teachers encourage and assist students to promote social change by reflecting on their values, their concerns for equitable society, and their willingness to participate in a more democratic community. In encouraging students' quest for social change through their addressing of social problems and their creating a better and more democratic society, I found it difficult to get them to challenge their own beliefs and values as far as race is concerned.

Students have problems acknowledging racial inequalities and the role they and I (and society at large) are playing in maintaining the social order. They do understand and passionately discuss inequalities related to gender and sexual orientation, as well as discrimination as it pertains to people with disabilities. However, as far as race is concerned, they develop a resistance that prevents them from challenging what is at stake. As a result of such reluctance, the safe place of dialogue becomes an arena of discomfort. My audacity and comfort of bringing such tough and hot topics in my used-to-be-safe classroom environment started being questioned. Students stopped or refused to participate in the classroom discussion and the dialogue turned to be a monologue.

As a Freirian, and an advocate of students' voices, I tried my best to recreate the safe space for students to open up and share their concerns through writing. Students were given the opportunity to anonymously write down what they think of the issue and what prevents them from openly discussing the issue of race as we used to do with other topics. To my surprise, many students took the problem personally as if I did it on purpose by bringing in the issue of race to make them feel embarrassed and to blame them. Some of them said they took my class in order to learn how to be good teachers, not to be political, nor to lose their time discussing old-fashioned issues. Others would go further, reminding me that race is no longer an issue (especially in Canada), but rather I am "the issue"; and if I am not happy, I just have to take my stuff and go back to where I come from.

They believe that there are many opportunities in North America allowing immigrants like me to enter the country and be successful. So, again, "race is no longer the issue." Students refuse to unpack the ambivalence of their historic and sociocultural values as far as race is concerned. Freire (2005) argued:

> Our relationship with learners demands that we respect them and demands equally that we be aware of the concrete conditions of their world, the conditions that shape them.... Without this, we have no access to the way they think, so only with great difficulty can we perceive what and how they know. (p. 79)

Therefore, I tried to understand their reactions and start where they are in order to better understand them while still challenging them. However, in comparison to my colleague's classroom, I wonder whether our race and ethnicity either facilitate or hamper students' understanding and action towards social justice and inequality.

The other issue I would like to raise is that of neoliberalism and globalization. According to McLaren (2002), only liberal or progressive education can challenge the neoliberal order by creating:

> "communities of learners" in classrooms, to bridge the gap between student culture and the culture of the school, to engage in cross-cultural understand-

ings, to integrate multicultural content and teaching across the curriculum, to develop techniques for reducing racial prejudice and conflict resolution strategies, to challenge Eurocentric teaching and history, to challenge the meritocratic foundation of public policy that purportedly is politically neutral and racially color-blind, to create teacher-generated narratives as a way of analyzing teaching from a "transformative" perspective, to improve academic achievement in culturally diverse schools, to affirm and utilize multiple perspectives and ways of teaching and learning, to de-reify the curriculum and to fight against exclusion. (p. 3)

Students had to answer to questions such as:

- Should teachers be international in their outlook?
- Shall they take a global perspective with problems? Why or why not?
- Can we think globally and act locally?

In addressing globalization, I tried to start from where the students are, by using Vygotsky's notion of zone of proximal development and Freire's focus on the importance of students' lived experiences. The class became again, as hooks said, "a place of ecstasy." We started then from what they know and what problems they see as far as globalization or international issues are concerned. Students started from their own international endeavors as Canadian students in American school. Many of my students are from Canada and have to commute from their Canadian city to the college almost every week. Since September 11, the American homeland security has tightened its laws and regulations. When entering the American borders, students have to present some specific papers such as their I-20 from the American school they are attending.

This, according to students, has been a hassle, and some of them have to go back to Canada or miss classes when they happen to forget any of these documents at home. Students shared their frustration every week and believed that border crossing is an international issue that needs to be less complicated in the 21st century, as we all live in a global village nowadays. Therefore, border crossing should be more flexible to promote internationalization and diversity.

I first sympathized with my students because as an alien, a legal immigrant in the American soil, I go through the same hassle whenever I travel abroad. Like the issue of gender, the issue of border crossing went smoothly without much tension. Even the few American students agree that the Canadian students deserve a better treatment at the border. However, my role as a facilitator is to challenge students' comfort zone. As I pressed students to consider whether Canada is not doing the same thing at its borders and if their advocacy for a more flexible border crossing rules includes other countries, the atmosphere changed. Among Americans and Canadians, things should go smoothly but they both have to protect their borders from intruders like me. Again I was seen as the "other" who is doing everything to embarrass her students or to put blame on their countries.

I moved to the next activity, as my purpose has been to help them see both sides (or multiple sides) of the picture. It consisted of reading and discussing Kincaid's (2000) book on colonization and tourism. This raised the issue of First World and Third World, the economic dependency as well as the political influence and the lingering neocolonialism in many poor countries. And again, it becomes North America against Africa, or the First World against the Third World. Students showed again their frustration of the choices of my readings, videos, and discussions. They believed that tourism has nothing to do with exploitation, and that the Third World countries should thank the "First World" for helping them develop their countries (via tourism) rather than blaming them. Again, students could not detach themselves and be more objective in their analysis. They were willing to talk about globalization but would not accept any neoliberal association with it.

To the question of whether teachers should be global and act local, students did refuse to see the link and the global dependency of countries, be it Third or First World. They insisted that teachers in North America have a lot to take care of and should not bother discussing other countries or issues of colonization, as it does not help them to be good teachers. Talking to my colleague helped me to reflect on the issues I faced, and continue to face, in my classroom. Students express their discomfort when I am challenging their assumptions and opinions. As for my Caucasian female colleague, her interest in the issue of race is considered to be "a passion." My status as a Black African woman, whose race, ethnicity, and language "with an accent" was what was seen to take precedence over my passion in education. I then became the "academic other" to avoid and earned the uncomplimentary nickname of "a mad black African woman" as reflected by a more than annoyed student in his or her end-of-semester evaluation of my teaching.

While hooks and other African American women deal with the issue of race in the classroom as well as in academia in general, my problem goes beyond the discourse of race and gender to include the issue of ethnicity. Hooks and others problematized the question of race in the classroom, yet the matter of ethnicity in the classroom remains undertheorized. We need to deconstruct the problem of power (in its different forms) and pedagogical relations in order to expose the hegemonic local and international discourses that prevent democratic teaching practices.

I refuse to support any "pedagogy of refusal or alienation" that would purposefully avoid creating tension in the classroom by not deconstructing issues of race and ethnicity among others. I advocate theorizing the impact/effects of the teacher's race, ethnicity, class, and gender in the classroom as a source of understanding, resistance and action, but also as a source of acceptance and surrender to the social order. This is one sure way to avoid situating students in a position of the "bewildered herd." Despite students' reluctance to challenge the social order and their own beliefs and values, we should find ways and means to reduce the tension and help them acknowledge their agency and their role as agents for social change/social reformers.

Another Professor's Classroom Experiences: "You're so *passionate* about these issues!" and "E-racing" whiteness

I will begin this section by providing a brief overview of my approach to the course and then follow it with two classroom anecdotes relating to students' perceptions of teacher–content synergy.

My teaching approach, as a White American professor, for "Critical Issues and Future Trends in Education" encourages students to employ various "theoretical lenses" (i.e., race, social class, gender, self-fulfilling prophecy) to "read" many critical issues in education (i.e., standardized test reform, charter schooling, voucher plans, religion vs. public schooling), analyzing and synthesizing relationships and speculating about how these lenses and issues might impact their future teaching experiences. While there is a weekly writing component involving theoretical analysis of educational issues, classroom meetings are primarily focused on facilitating a Freirean (1970, 2005) approach to peer interaction, in that students are encouraged to debate about issues and "make meaning" in relation to frequently difficult theoretical concepts and contentious educational issues.

In order to assist students in what is typically a very difficult transition into theoretical thought and practice, classroom activities are designed to link theory explored in the weekly readings, personal educational experiences, and teaching approaches. Since this course meets only once per week for a little under three hours, these interactions become paramount in terms of addressing misunderstandings and promoting a familiarity with theoretical language and theory–practice connections.

My first anecdote revolves around students' viewing of *Children in America's Schools* during the second or third week of the course. Briefly, this video is based on Kozol's (1991) book *Savage Inequalities*, and it provides multiple starkly contrasted schooling environments throughout the United

States during the early 1990s, analyzing perspectives of students and teachers from wealthy suburban schools, as well as those from impoverished urban and rural schools. Although my students, as noted above, are predominantly White Canadians—who more experienced professors have highlighted as a group rejecting Canadian poverty levels as real and in existence—my students do not reject the possibility of this level of poverty in their Canadian educational system as their predecessors have in the past. Part of this has to do with their awareness of shifting student populations, with greater numbers of impoverished and/or immigrant populations moving into urban centers like Toronto, as well as long-held racist perceptions of areas like "Jane and Finch" (a highly impoverished area recently central to an all-Black school proposal and debate).

However, their acceptance of this inequality and desire to address it in their classrooms is accompanied by exclamations by my "passion" about such issues, and my intellectual and physical "availability" to field their questions, both as a group and individually. Some students have even asked for copies of the DVD, as they wish to share it with their family, friends, and teachers in whose classrooms they are currently observing. Finally, although I accompany our conversations and viewings surrounding such educational inequalities with concrete approaches to addressing them (i.e., organizing classrooms and activities according to Gardner's (1993) theory of multiple intelligences rather than fostering ability grouping and tracking), I am left wondering if students are instead remaining at the first step of encouraging awareness among colleagues and friends.

This, unfortunately, would lead to fostering an approach detached from action, akin to what Groves (2002) found with her White preservice students who, upon viewing the very same video, determined that the solution was showing all White and/or privileged people the video and raising awareness.

A second anecdote that helps concretize my perceived status as "passionate" transformed into an acceptance of my authoritarian control over their behavior in the classroom is in relation to Foucault's (1977) theory of Panopticism. During the 11th week of the semester (and only a few weeks from the end of it), students read excerpts from Foucault about Panopticism and how it relates to the surveillance and self-surveillance that occurs in American and Canadian societies. As with many of my other classes, before we discuss the material and begin the process of "meaning making," I present a few PowerPoint slides of pertinent definitions that we might consider during said conversation, the first of which is Panopticism. In order to mobilize a few other of Gardner's multiple intelligences (notably, spatial and bodily-kinesthetic), I ask a few students to stand at their seats (which are already organized in a U-shape, as they are every other week in order to facilitate conversations), while one student sits in a chair at the center of the students. I point out that the student in the center reflects the tower in the Panopticon, while those standing at their seats represent individual cells, as well as the fact that no one need be in the tower at any point, as the individual cells can not see into it and must assume someone is there, behaving accordingly.

In one of the sections of this course during this slide presentation, one of my White Canadian female students (who also developed an intense interest in Foucault's work through this course and others throughout the semester), cried: "Why are you listening to her? Why are you doing what she's telling you to do?" Her peers began laughing, but I quickly acted on this (unexpected) "teachable moment" to point out that she had not only illustrated a break with blindly acting out Foucault's self-surveilling behavior, but she had also integrated Freire's approaches into her outburst, understanding the oppressive construction of the classroom and *acting* on that realization (thereby linking reflection and action). *Nowhere* in this or any of the other conversations with any of my course sections did my students, American or Canadian, question that I was pointing out this inequality or those dealing specifically with race in light of my own Whiteness.

Further, although I am a White American woman with blonde hair, *none* of my students in these course sections have linked our Steinberg (1997) reading about Barbie (*The Bitch Who Has Everything*) to my appearance, instead drawing from celebrities or even other students in the classroom for visual examples. As an educational researcher, my observational radar was cranked to the breaking point during classroom meetings in which we discussed race and gender-related issues with Barbie, and the absence of my race and gender linked to these issues was deafening. Ultimately, what I heard repeatedly from my students was that my "passion," my "drive," my "focus" on these issues proved central to harnessing their attention—and all as divorced from direct links to my identity as a White American woman.

Synthesizing Racialized Teaching Perspectives

Our two discourses in the classroom are based on the pedagogy of empowerment that promotes an understanding and action: understanding of the relationships between power and knowledge and action for a more democratic society. Students' reactions to the readings that talk about the historic and present role of race in education and in the classroom (Christensen and Karp's introduction to *Rethinking School*, 2003; Kozol's article "Still Separate, Still Unequal"; as well as the documentary *Children in America's Schools*) were different from one class to the other. As we have shown, students' awareness seems to be impacted by the class, ethnicity, and race of their professors. Even though some of them in the second professor's class moved towards a certain level of awareness, the first professor's students, on the contrary, were still at the stage of questioning (and/or frustration with) the relevance of such realities of race and racial inequalities in today's school.

Further, even students' attitudes toward the two professors' very similar style of facilitating consistent questioning of racial issues reflected their racially laden perspectives, in that they viewed the second professor as "passionately" pursuing social justice, whereas the first professor manifests the standpoint of "a mad black African woman." We are struck by the overwhelming notion that students respond more positively to a decentering of their racialized worlds when it is "packaged" in white skin, begging the question as to whether or not they are seriously undertaking perspectival transformations in the second professor's classroom at all.

CONCLUDING THOUGHTS, IMPLICATIONS AND PATHS FOR FUTURE RESEARCH

We hope that this work will foster conversations among educators, and between educators and students, about the importance of multicultural approaches to critical issues in classrooms. Further, we specifically hope to contribute to ongoing conversations regarding critical pedagogy, as well as racial and gender issues, as they pertain to teacher identity formation processes in teacher education programs.

REFERENCES

Anzaldua, G. (1987). *Borderlands/La frontera: The new mestiza*. San Francisco, CA: Aunt Lute Books.

Christensen, L. & Karp, S. (2003). *Rethinking school reform: View from the classroom*. Milwaukee, WI: Rethinking Schools Press.

Foucault, M. (1998). Method. In J. Storey (Ed.), *Cultural theory & popular culture: A reader*. Athens, GA: University of Georgia Press.

Freire, P. (1970). *Pedagogy of the oppressed*. New York, NY: Continuum.

Freire, P. (2005). *Teachers as cultural workers*. MA: Westview Press.

Giroux, H. A. (1994). *Disturbing pleasures: Learning popular culture*. New York, NY: Routledge.

Hayes, M. T., & Groves, P. (2002). The medium is the experience: Uses of media in multicultural education. *Multicultural Education, 10*(2), 15–18.

hooks, b. (1994). *Teaching to transgress: Education as the practice of freedom*. New York, NY: Routledge.

Kincaid, J. (2000). *A small place*. New York, NY: Farrar, Straus and Giroux.

Kincheloe, J. (2005). *Critical pedagogy*. New York, NY: Peter Lang.

Kozol, J. (1991). *Savage inequalities: Children in America's schools*. New York, NY: Crown.

Ladson-Billings, G. J. (1995). Toward a critical race theory of education. *Teachers College Record*, *97*, 47–68.

Tate, W. F. (1997). Critical race theory and education: History, theory, and implications. *Review of Research in Education*, *22*, 195–247.

AUTHOR QUERIES:

On manuscript p. 3, you cite Foucault (1981), but the only work you have listed by Foucault in your references has a date of 1998. Is that what you meant to cite? The 1998 work is not cited elsewhere, so if that's what you're citing here, please check the date and make the citation and reference match.

On ms p. 7, you cite McLaren (2002), but it is not in your references. Please add.

Please list *Children in America's Schools*, cited on ms p. 12, in your references.

On ms p. 13, you cite Gardner (1993), Groves (2002), and Foucault (1977), but they are not in your references. Please add.

On ms p. 15, you cite Steinberg (1997), but it is not in your references. Please add.

Please add Kozol's article "Still Separate, Still Unequal"; as well as the documentary *Children in America's Schools*, referenced on ms p. 15, to your references.

ABOUT THE AUTHORS

Barrel Gueye/Mrs. Abeidi is a passionate of human rights, social justice and quality education for ALL with numerous years of in-depth and well-rounded expertise in teaching and research; she is also an advocate for women's empowerment. Dr. Gueye-Abeidi has experiences at all levels of the education cycle including extensive teaching experience at the University level, especially in the United States. Dr. Gueye's areas of expertise include research appraisal and program management and coordination. Dr. Gueye is currently the Senior Policy Manager of The African Sanitation Think Tank in Water and Sanitation for Africa in Burkina Faso, West Africa. Her work consists of promoting "evidence for policy & action" to impact change and enhance the sustainability of sanitation projects in Africa using evidence-based research to address and fnfluence policy and practice at scale. Consequently she is in charge of creating the platform to simulate intellectual debates, identify policy and practice gaps, raise the profile of innovations and best practices in sanitation.

Van Z. Ciupak is an Assistant Professor in the Department of Sociology and Anthropology at Northern Michigan University. Her publication includes book chapters, articles, and a book on social class and education, sociology of education theories, and immigrant experience. Her new book, *On the Nexus of Local and Global: Chinese Higher Education and College Students in the Era of Globalization,* will be published by AMC Press.

Esther Somé-Guiébré is currently a lecturer at the University of Koudougou in Burkina Faso (West Africa). She holds a PhD in Curriculum and Instruction from the University of Illinois. She conducted a qualitative study on the challenges faced by francophone immigrant students in American students. Her research interest covers multicultural education, postcolonialism, immigration issues, and gender issues. Email: someesther@gmail.com

Carl E. James is Director of the York Centre for Education and Community (YCEC), and Professor in the Faculty of Education and Graduate Programs in Sociology and Social Work at York University, Toronto, Canada. A former Affirmative Action Officer for the university, his research interests include examination of issues of equity and social justice pertaining to access, inclusion and retention of racialized individuals in education and employment. A Fellow of the Academy of Social Sciences of the Royal Society of Canada, one of his most recent publications is: *Life at the Intersection: Community, Class and Schooling* (2012).

Catherine Lalonde is an Assistant Professor of Education and NCATE Coordinator at D'Youville College. She teaches "Critical Issues and Future Trends in Education," "Multiculturalism and Cultural Diversity," and "Research in Education" and her research interests include multicultural theory, social foundations of education, food distribution and consumption issues, and critical media literacy and pedagogy. Email: lalondec2@dyc.edu, lalondeorama@gmail.com

Muna J. Shami is a senior research analyst whose research and evaluation efforts seek to improve the lives of children, youth, and their families by bridging research, policy, and practice. Her research interests include foundations of education, critical pedagogy, and how arts, culture, and education empower individual and collective transformation. She holds masters degrees in Counseling and Developmental Psychology and earned her doctorate in Education Studies from American University (Dissertation: *Towards a Critical Pedagogy of Possibility: Hip Hop and Spoken Word by Arab-Americans as Cultural Action for Freedom*).

Guofang Li is an Associate Professor of second language and literacy education in the Department of Teacher Education, Michigan State University. Li's research focuses on immigrant students' home literacy practices and their relationships to schooling framed around issues of culture, race, class, and gender; Asian immigrants' education, their social processes of learning, the impact of the "model minority" myth on language and literacy development; and research-based practices in ESL/EFL education. Li is the recipient of the 2011 Publication Award of the Association of Chinese Professors of Social Sciences in the U.S. (ACPSS), the 2010 Early Career Award at American Educational Research Association (AERA), the 2008 Division G Early Career Award of AERA, and the 2006 Ed Fry Book Award of the National Reading Conference (NRC). Li has published 9 books and over 60 journal articles and book chapters. Her recent works include *Handbook of Asian Education: A Cultural Approach* (Routledge, 2011); *Best Practices in ELL Instruction* (2010, Guilford Press). *Multicultural Families, Home Literacies, and Mainstream Schooling* (2009, IAP), *Model Minority Myths Revisited: An Interdisciplinary Approach to Demystifying Asian American Education Experiences* (2008, IAP), and *Culturally Contested Literacies: America's "rainbow underclass" and Urban Schools* (2008, Routledge), which just won the 2013 Ed Fry Book Award from the Literary Research Association (LRA). Li teaches undergraduate, graduate, and doctoral courses in second language literacy education at MSU.

Betty Okwako, a native of Kenya, teaches in the Department of Teacher Education at Michigan State University. Dr. Okwako holds a doctorate in Curriculum, Instruction and Teacher Education from Michigan State University. She previously earned her Master's in International Development from Western Michigan University. Her Bachelor's degree was in Education with a minor in Business Studies and French from Kenyatta University in Kenya. Her areas of interest include immigrant education, social foundations of education, international development, comparative and international education and issues related to gender in education.

Marisol Ruiz is an Assistant Professor at Humboldt State University in the School of Education. She earned her PhD in Language Literacy and Culture, emphasis in Educational Thought and Cultural Studies from the University of New Mexico. Dr. Ruiz specializes in Bilinguai/TESOL Education, which includes language education, biliteracy, multiliteracy, multicultural education, teacher education, critical pedagogy, participatory action research, teacher action research, and youth social movements. Dr. Ruiz's research focus is on Critical Social Justice Bilingual I TESOL Pedagogies that lead to youth organization.

Touorizou Hervé Somé is a Fulbright scholar who has studied education policy at the University of Buffalo, NY, where he earned his PhD in 2007. He has published several peer-reviewed book chapters and journal articles addressing education reform and higher education finance in Africa. Other research interests include globalization, neoliberalism, alternative forms of education, gender bias in education, qualitative research, and teacher preparation in developing countries. He is currently an associate professor at Ripon College, Wisconsin, where he teaches social and philo-sophical foundations of education, contemporary, issues in Africa and its diaspora, English as a Second Language, and supervises student teachers in their field placements. Email: thsome63@yahoo.com

Pierre Orelus, a poet, a former high school teacher, Dr. Pierre Wilbert Orelus, is associate professor in the Curriculum and Instruction depart-ment at New Mexico State University (NMSU) where he co-coordinated and coordinated the Bilingual and TESOL program for over two years. Orelus has published eight books and numerous peer reviewed articles and book chapters since completing his doctorate from University of Mas-sachusetts-Amherst in 2008. In praising Dr. Orelus for his book, *The Agony of Masculinity,* the acclaimed African American public intellectual Cornel West stated, "Orelus is an intellectual freedom fighter whose deep insights and sharp analyses of institutional racism and black masculinity deserve our attention." Dr. Orelus is currently the Co-Chair of the Paulo Freire SIG (Special Interest Group) and the past Chair of the postcolonial and Education SIG at American Educational Research Association. Professor Orelus's research interests include the politics of language, race, gender, and culture studies; "postcolonial," and immigrant/transnational studies, biliteracy, and critical pedagogy. Dr. Orelus has been invited both as a guest and keynote speaker by major national conferences, such as CABE (California Association of Bilingual Education), and several U.S. colleges and universities, such as Mount-Holyoke College, Bates College, Keene State College, and University of Massachusetts at Amherst, to talk about his work.

CPSIA information can be obtained at www.ICGtesting.com
Printed in the USA
LVOW04s2358100715

445842LV00007B/38/P